How to

Microsoft

FrontPage 2002

Other Titles of Interest

How to Use

Microsoft

FrontPage 2002

David Weale

Bernard Babani (publishing) Ltd
The Grampians
Shepherds Bush Road
London W6 7NF
England
www.babanibooks.com

Please Note

All rights reserved

© 2002 BERNARD BABANI (publishing) LTD

First Published – September 2002

British Library Cataloguing in Publication Data

A catalogue record for this book is available from the British Library

ISBN 0 85934 5289

Cover Design by Gregor Arthur

Printed and bound in Great Britain by Cox and Wyman Ltd

Preface

Welcome, I wrote this book to help you in learning how to use the program in a practical way. It is intended to explain the program in a way that I hope you will find useful.

FrontPage is a web page and web site design program, which makes it easy to design and structure web sites. It can be used in a relatively simple manner but it is also a professional tool and is capable of creating very sophisticated sites.

Each section of the book covers a different aspect of the program and contains various hints and tips which I have found useful and may enhance your work.

There are tutorial sections dealing with HTML and FrontPage 2002 as well as explanations of the program features, the basics of web design and a glossary.

The text is written both for the new user and for the more experienced person who wants an easy to follow reference.

You should know how to use the basic techniques of Microsoft® Windows®; if you do not, there are many excellent texts on the subject.

I hope you learn from this book and have fun doing so.

David Weale, September 2002

Trademarks

About the author

David Weale is a Fellow of the Institute of Chartered Accountants and has worked in both private and public practice. At present, he is a lecturer in business computing.

Contents

Starting Off

The Views Bar

When you initially load the program you will see the following screen with the **Views** bar shown on the left (use the buttons on the **Views** bar to look at your work in different ways).

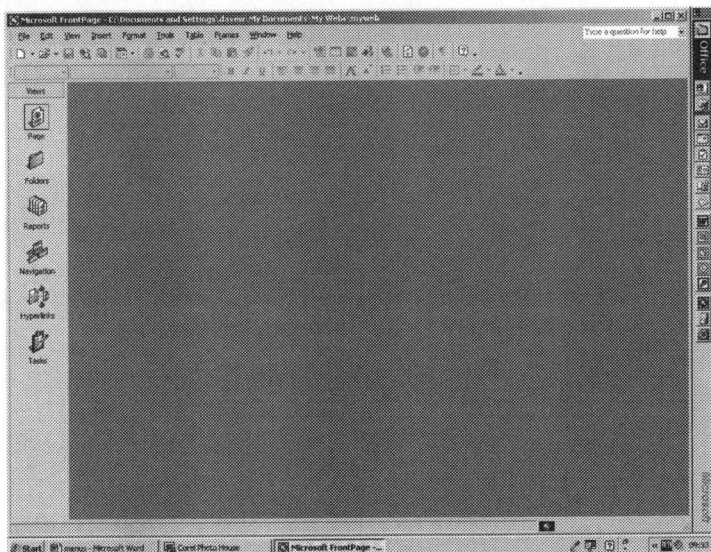

To start

To start a new web, click the *arrow* to the right of the **New** button and select **Web**.

Select the type of web, e.g. *Empty Web,* and alter the **location** to which the web will be saved if you wish.

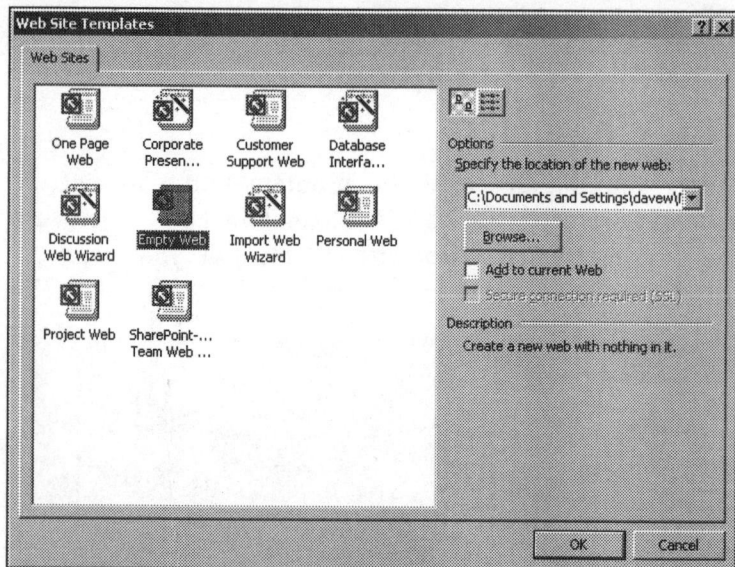

Once the web has been started, to create a home page, click the **Navigation** button on the **Views** toolbar and then click the **New** button and the home page of your web will be ready.

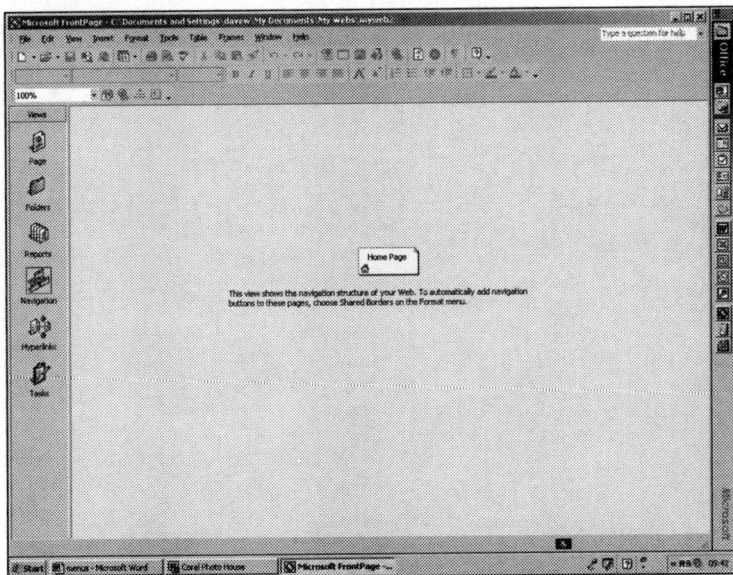

Double-click the *Home Page* icon and the actual page will
appear in the editor so that data can be entered.

You can display a list of the files and folders in the current web by clicking the **Folders** button on the **Views** toolbar.

The relative size of the work area, folder list and **Views** bar can be adjusted by clicking and dragging the dividing line.

The Views toolbar

The different views are described below.

Page

Use this to look at individual pages. To load a page, double-click it in **Navigation** or **Folders** view.

Folders

This displays the folders and files contained within the selected folder.

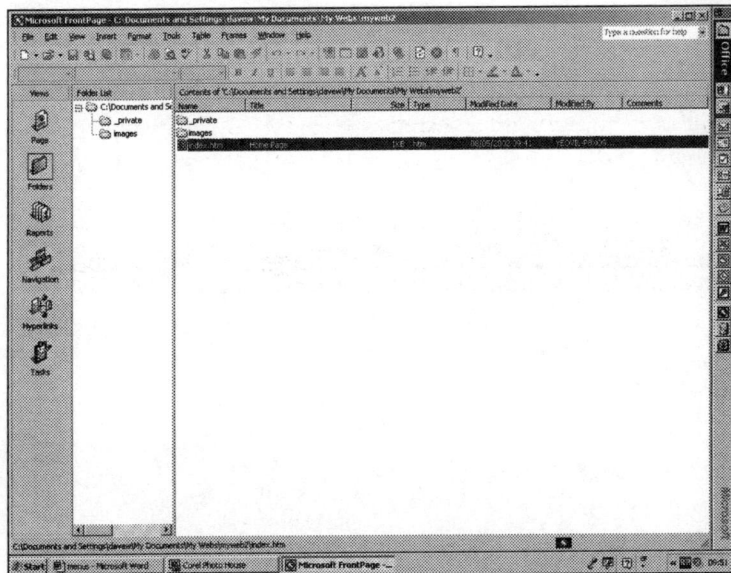

Reports

The *Site Summary* report displays information about your web, e.g. the number and sizes of files and pictures, hyperlinks, number of incomplete tasks and so on.

Navigation

This shows the structure of the web, how the pages are linked together.

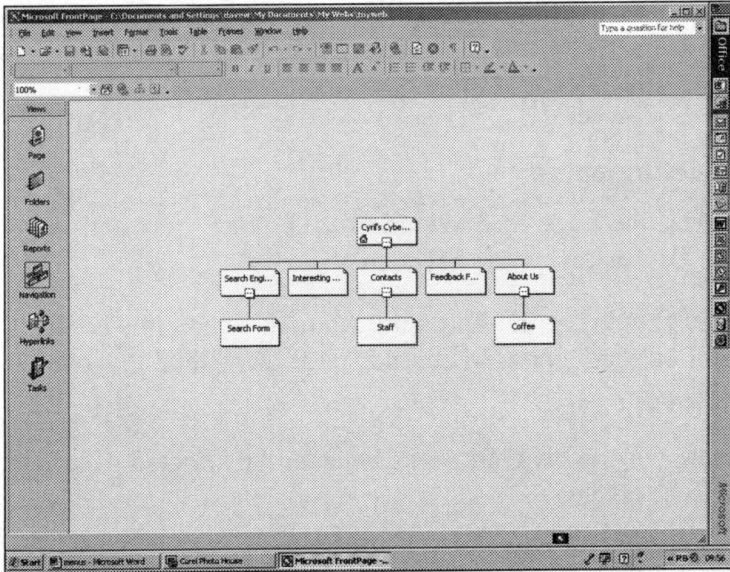

In this view you can add pages to the site, delete pages and move pages around by dragging and dropping (i.e. alter the relationship between the pages).

One of the major advantages of the program is that all the hyperlinks between the pages are normally changed when you alter the relationship between them (if you have added navigation bars to your pages).

Adding pages

You can add a new page to one of the existing pages by selecting an existing page (click the page in **Navigation** view) and clicking on the **New Page** button.

This adds the page below the existing page.

Deleting pages

Select the page in **Navigation** or **Folder view** and press the **Delete** key on the keyboard.

You should see the following warning screen (the contents will depend upon where the page is within the overall structure).

Note what it says; all pages beneath the selected page will also be deleted.

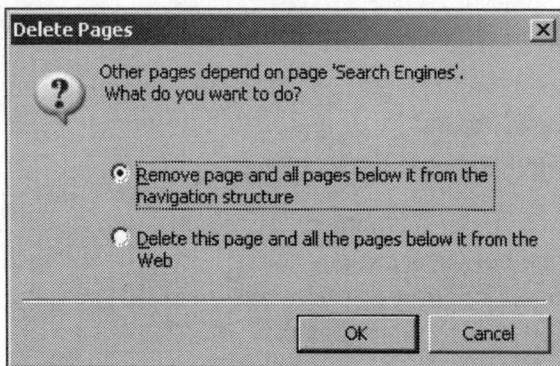

The first option removes the page(s) from the **Navigation Bars**, but leaves the page(s) within the site so that they can be put back by dragging from the **Folder List** and positioning within the structure. The second option removes them from the web entirely.

Moving pages

Like most programs, FrontPage uses **drag** and **drop** to move files. This means that you select the page (by clicking on it) and then drag it to a new position.

As you drag it you will see (joining) lines appear, when you have moved it to the correct position simply let go of the mouse button.

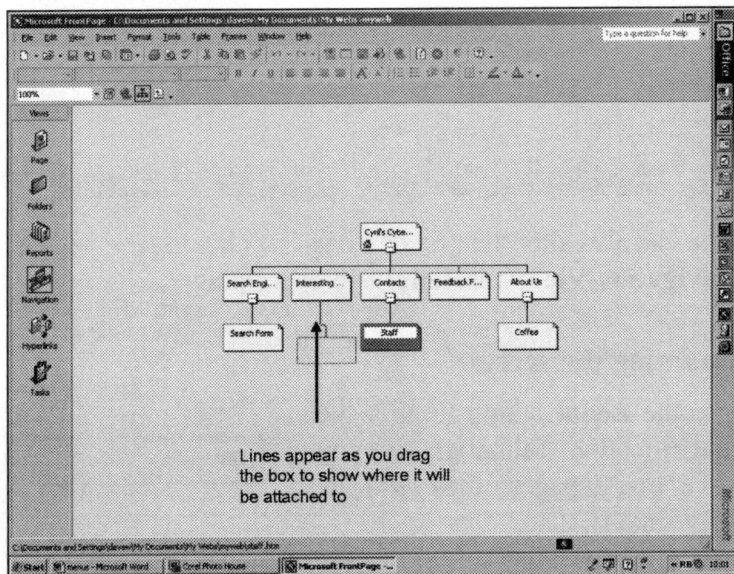

Renaming files and pages

You can rename a file by clicking the page, right-clicking the mouse and selecting **Rename**.

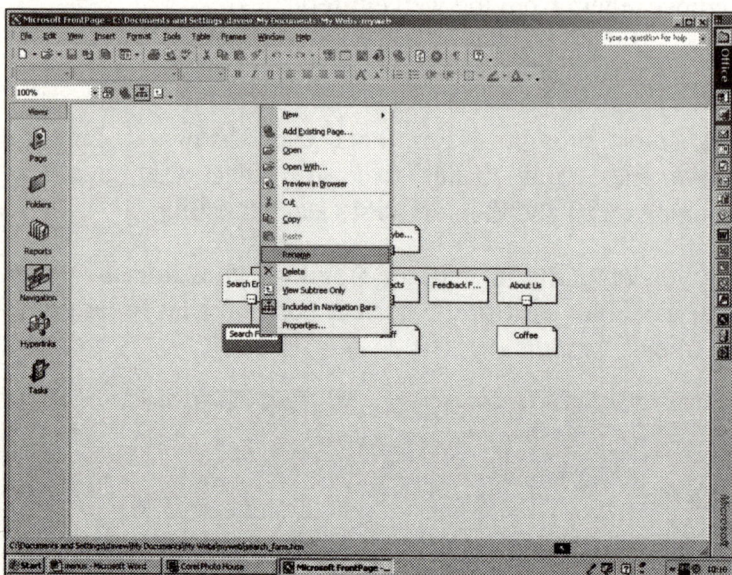

You can also alter the title of a page by clicking the page in **Navigation View** (carefully) and overtyping.

Zooming the screen

Use the **Zoom** button to alter the magnification (although if you have many pages, they will be very small!).

Hyperlinks

This shows the hyperlinks to/from a selected
page (you select the file using the **Folder List**).

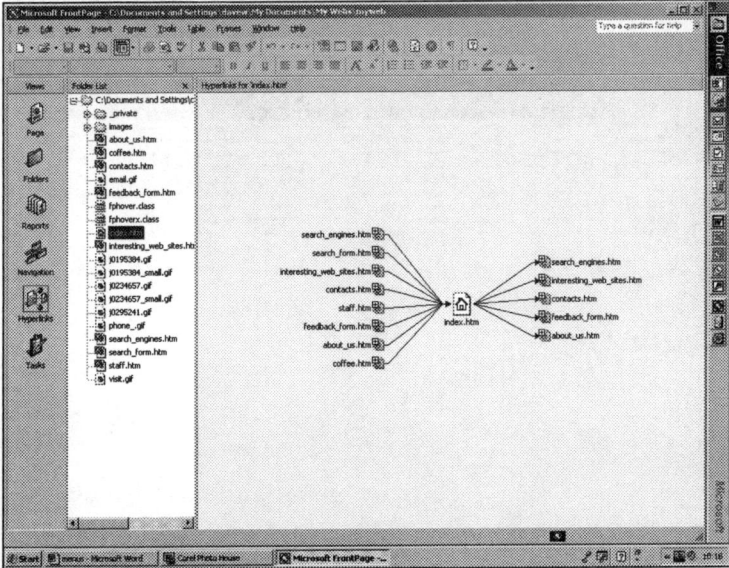

Tasks

This shows a history of all tasks or uncompleted tasks, right-click the mouse to deal with the task.

Alternatively, double-click a task and the following dialog box will appear, from which the task can be started.

Task Details		? X

Priority
- ○ High
- ● Medium
- ○ Low

Task name: `Fix misspelled words`

Assigned to: `davew` ▼

Associated with: search_engines.htm

Completed: No

Modified by: (Has not been modified)

Created by: davew (FrontPage's Spelling) on 10/05/2002 at 15:49:25

Description:

Misspelled words: david weale

[Start Task] [OK] [Cancel]

FrontPage Tutorial

This contains practical exercises in creating a web site that use many of the features of **FrontPage**.

Please be aware that this is a learning exercise and different techniques will be looked at. The pages, therefore, may not have a consistency of layout and style that you would want on your web site.

When you create your own site the most important factor in your success (or not) is the amount of effort and care you put into **planning** the site.

This means deciding upon the content of the pages, the way in which the pages relate to each other (structure) and so on.

You should do this before going near **FrontPage**.

Beginnings

Before starting check if you are working in 800*600 resolution. Many web pages are designed to look best in this resolution (use the **Control Panel**, and **Display**, **Settings** and **Screen Resolution** to alter the resolution).

After loading **FrontPage**, click the arrow to the right of the **New** button and choose **Web**.

Now choose the **Empty Web** option (shown in the illustration) - the new web will be saved automatically to a folder (which can be changed if desired).

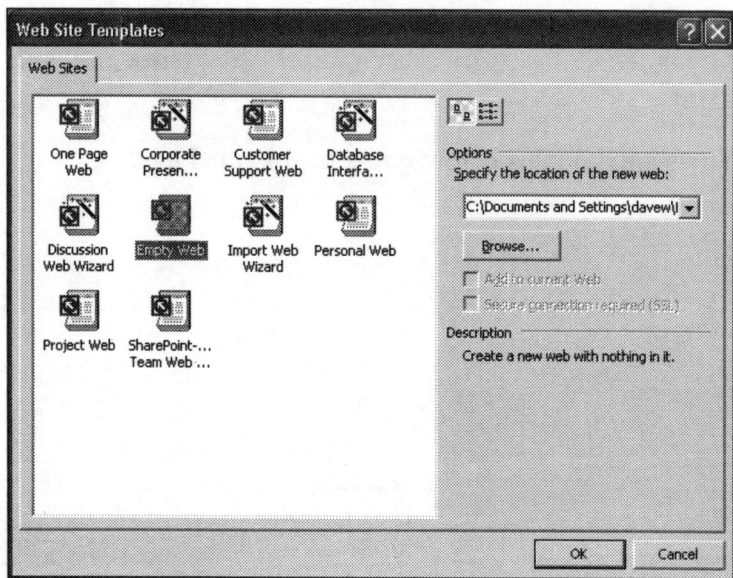

Click the **Navigation** button to make sure you are in navigation view.

Click the **New Page** button to create a **Home Page**.

If necessary, click the **Folder List** button on the toolbar (to hide the list of folders and files) so that you have more of the page visible.

The screen should now look like this.

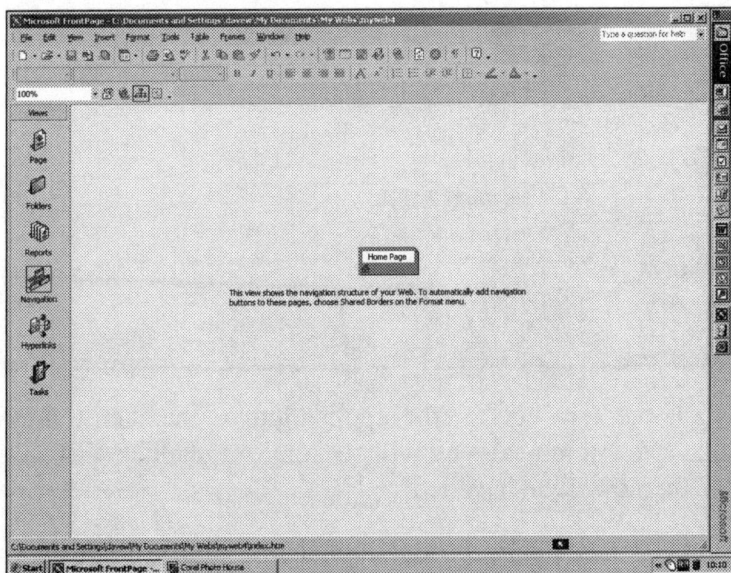

Themes

The first task is to apply a theme to your web. Pull down the **Format** menu and select **Theme**. Apply the **Blocks** theme and ensure the first three items (**Vivid Colors**, etc.) are selected (ticked).

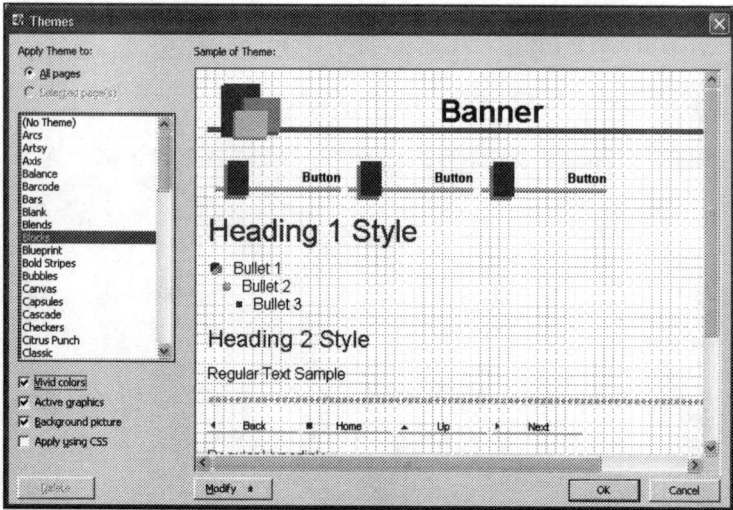

Click the **OK** button (the application of the theme may take a few minutes), you will see a message, click **Yes** and the theme will be installed.

When it has finished, double-click the **Home Page** icon and you will see the empty page.

Shared Borders

You are also going to include **Top** and **Bottom** borders for the pages in the web (you can add or remove borders for individual pages).

Pull down the **Format** menu and select **Shared Borders**, select **Top** and **Bottom** borders (as shown in the illustration - making sure the **Include navigation buttons** box is **not** ticked).

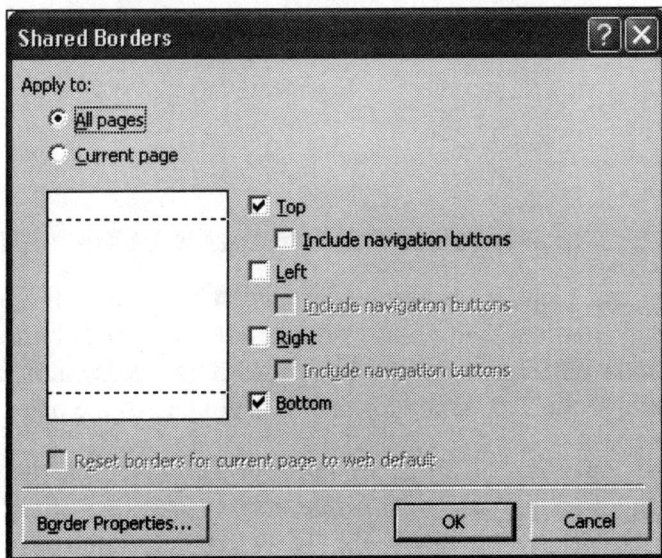

You should now see a page with the borders in place.

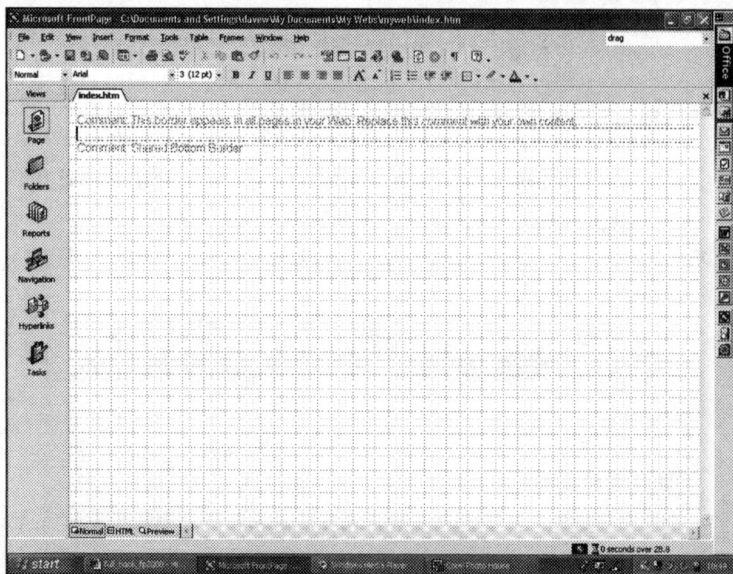

Note the page is in three sections, the top and bottom shared borders (anything within the top and bottom sections will appear on every page of the web) and the middle section, which is for the main content of the page.

Make sure the cursor is in the top section of the page, highlight all the text *within that section* and then insert a banner by pulling down the **Insert** menu, followed by **Page Banner**.

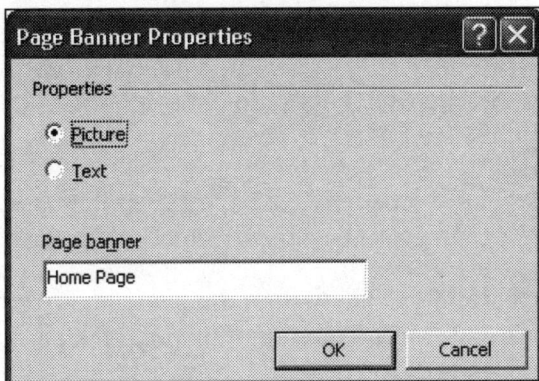

Page Banner Properties

Properties

- ( ) Picture
- ( ) Text

Page banner

Home Page

OK   Cancel

Make sure the settings are as shown above and you should see the following screen.

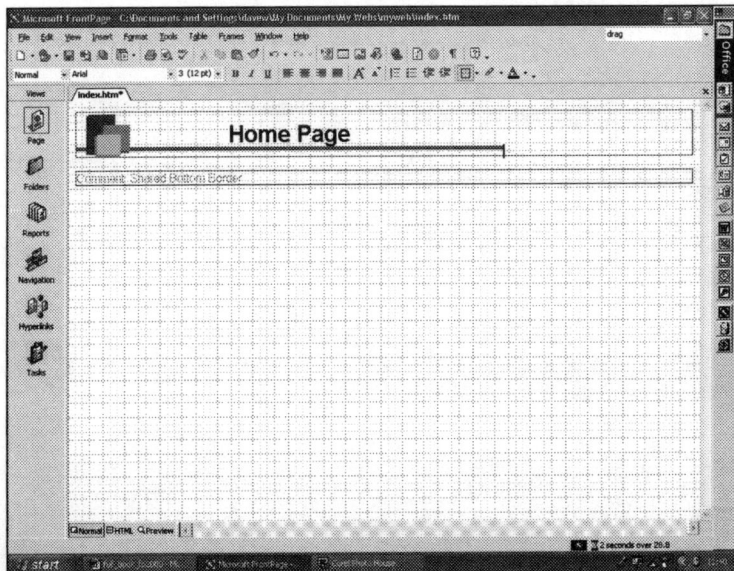

Renaming

Click the **Navigation** button (on the left of the screen in the **Views Bar**).

You are going to rename the page by changing *Home Page* to a more meaningful title (the title appears on the banner).

You can (carefully) click within the name and overtype (or **right-click** and select **Rename**), renaming the page:

Cyril's Cyber Cafe

If you double-click the icon you will see the title change within the page.

Finally centre the banner by selecting it and using the **Center** button on the toolbar.

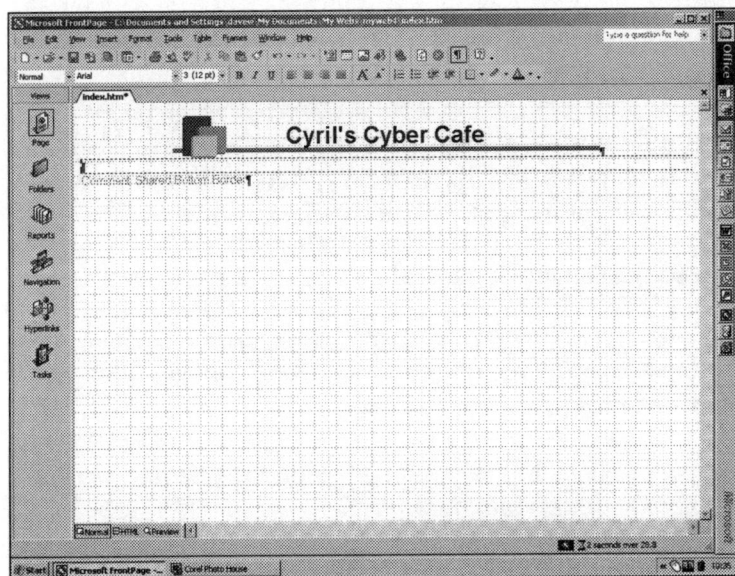

Adding text

Ensure the cursor is in the middle section and enter the following text, using the **Return** key to create a new paragraph after the title and between the paragraphs.

If you do not want a full **Return**, hold down the **Shift** key and then press the **Return** key, this will create a new paragraph but the gap will be smaller).

Welcome To Our Cyber Cafe

This site is made up of various pages, some explaining the services we offer, others advertising artistic and other services offered by our members.

Below are links to the other pages on the site and we hope you enjoy our endeavours.

Click within the first line (the heading) and pull down the **Style** box on lower toolbar, selecting **Heading 2** from the list.

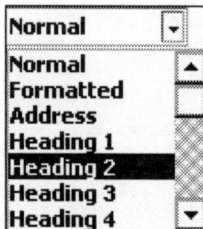

Now centre the heading, (using the **Center** button on the toolbar).

Highlight the remaining text you typed in and colour it dark blue (using the arrow to the right of the toolbar button).

Create space above the heading and below the bottom line of text (use the **Return** key).

Save your file (use the **Save** button), your page should look like this.

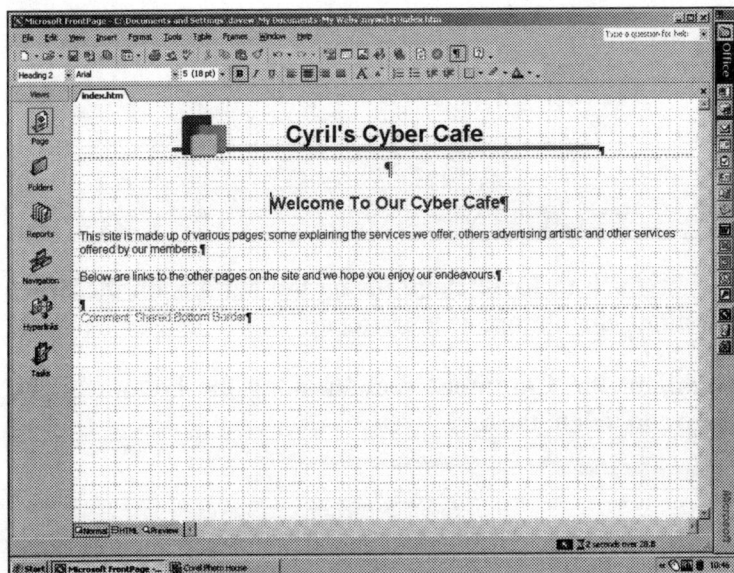

Click the **Preview in Browser** button and make the browser window full-screen.

You should see something like this (depending upon the browser you are using).

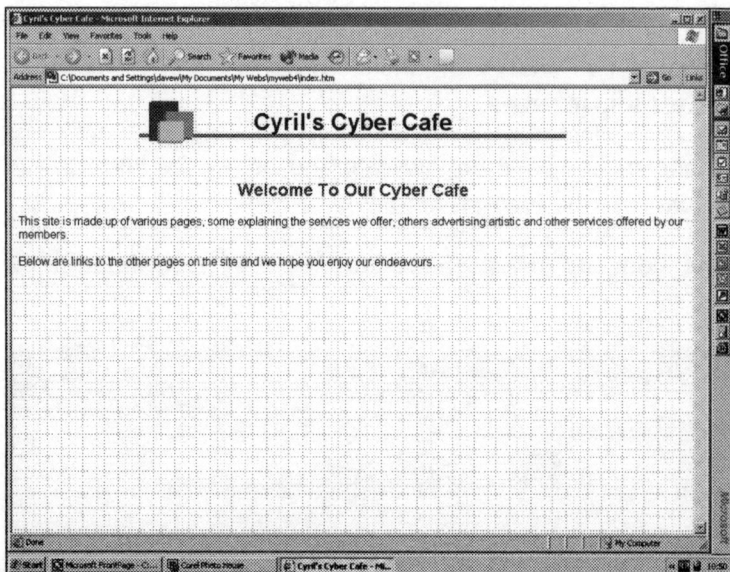

Switch back to **FrontPage** (using the buttons on the **Start** bar along the bottom of the screen).

Highlight the **Comment** section along the bottom of the page and delete the text.

Pull down the **Insert** menu and **Symbol**.

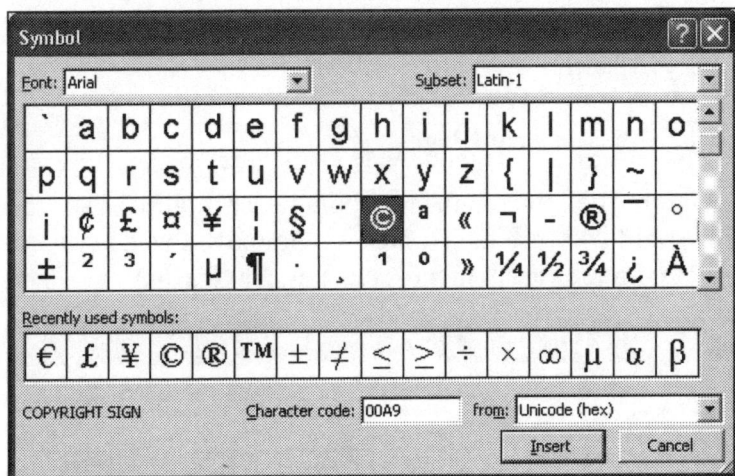

Insert the © symbol and close the dialog box.

Add your *name* and the *year*; format this to italic, 8-point size and red colour (**Format**, **Font** or use the toolbar buttons), finally centre it.

This will appear on all the pages as it is within the bottom shared border.

Save the file and switch to the browser, remember you must click the **Refresh** button to ensure that the saved changes are displayed.

Inserting (hyper) links

We now need to insert links to the other pages we are going to create.

Switch back to **FrontPage**.

Position the cursor in the bottom section, above the copyright text (use the **Return** key to move this down) and pull down the **Insert** menu, selecting **Navigation**.

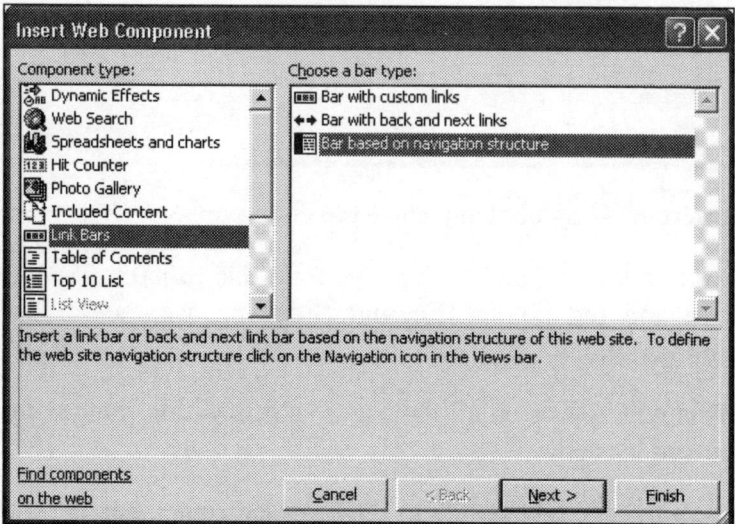

Make sure the settings are the same as the illustrations.

The next screen enables you to alter the **Theme**.

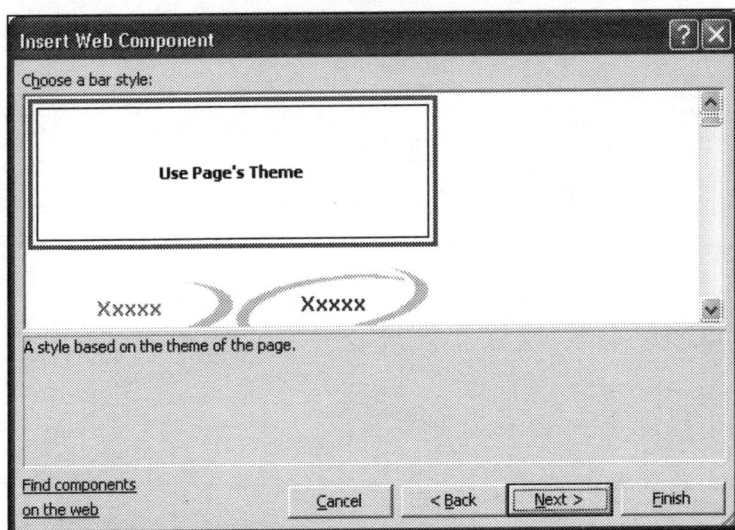

Accept this and continue.

This is followed by the choice of **Orientation**.

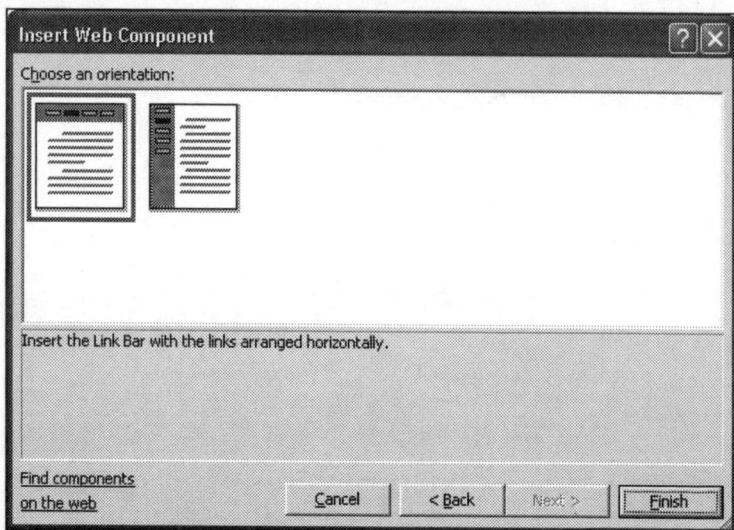

Accept this and click the **Finish** button.

The next stage is to decide upon the links, select the **Home** and **Parent** pages shown below.

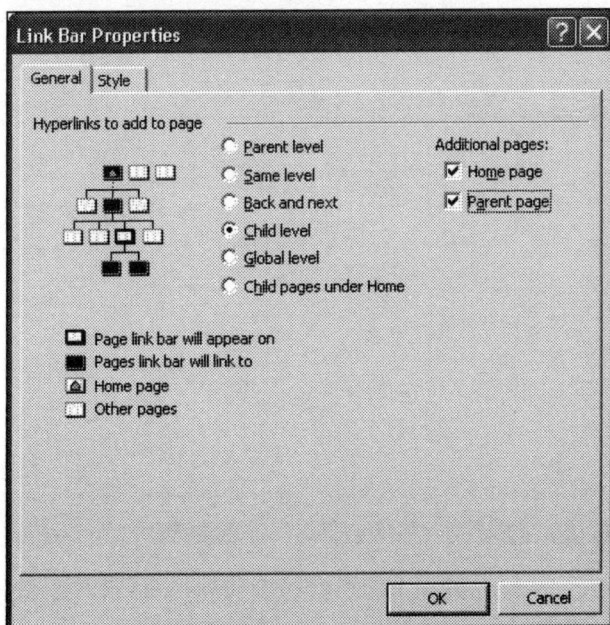

Link Bar Properties

General | Style

Hyperlinks to add to page

- ○ Parent level
- ○ Same level
- ○ Back and next
- ⦿ Child level
- ○ Global level
- ○ Child pages under Home

Additional pages:
- ☑ Home page
- ☑ Parent page

- ☐ Page link bar will appear on
- ■ Pages link bar will link to
- 🏠 Home page
- ☐ Other pages

OK   Cancel

The final result will look like this.

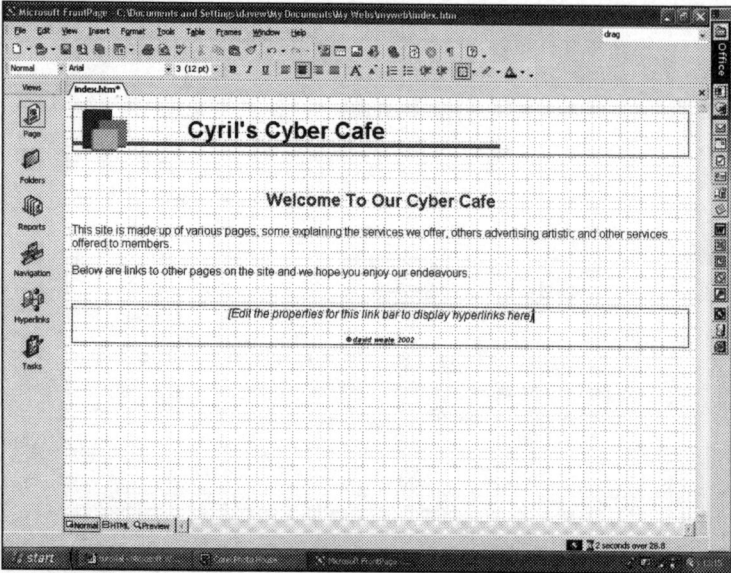

Select the navigation bar text and centre it on the page (if necessary).

Save the page and **Preview** it in the browser (remembering to **Refresh**).

The navigation bar hyperlinks will **not** appear until you have created additional pages in your web to link to.

Switch back to **FrontPage**.

Adding new pages

Click the **Navigation** button and add a new page by clicking the **New** button, dragging the page to a position beneath the original page (although if you selected the original page before adding the new page, this will happen automatically).

Alter the title by highlighting the text or **right clicking** and choosing **Rename**.

Search Engines

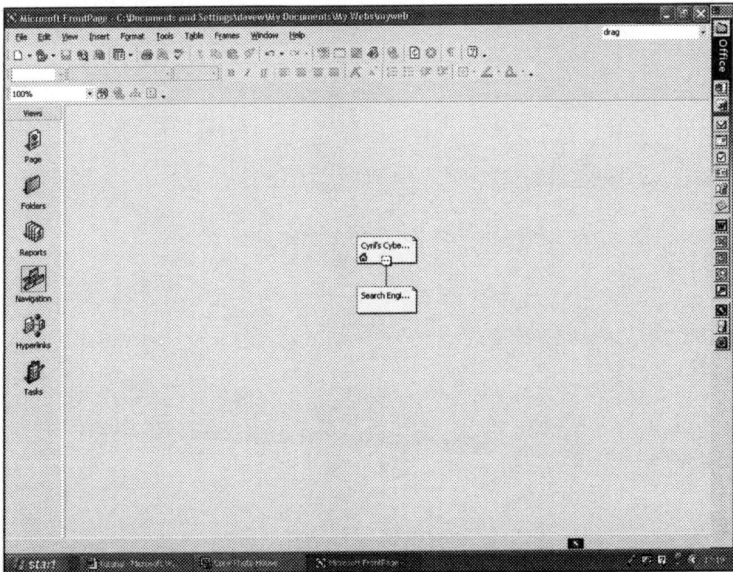

Double-click the page and you will see it on the screen.

Add the following text in the middle section of the page.

We have found the following search engines useful tools in finding information on the Internet.

You should become familiar with any one of these before experimenting as each engine works slightly differently. It is useful to print out the **Help** screens to gain a good understanding of how each engine works; in particular the ways in which to construct searches.

Use the **Return** key to add a space before and after the text.

Tables

You are now going to add a table with text and hyperlinks within it.

Position the cursor below the text and create a table (2 rows and 2 columns) by pulling down the **Table** menu and **Insert** followed by **Table** (alternatively use the **Table** button on the toolbar and select the cells).

Enter the following text (size to 10 point) into the first column.

Yahoo has two ways of searching, by category or by keyword.	
AltaVista is a more traditional search engine, enabling you to carry out both simple and more complex searches; it also has useful help screens.	

Hyperlinks and hover buttons

Now place the cursor in the top cell in the second column and using the **Insert** and **Web Component** insert a **Hover Button**.

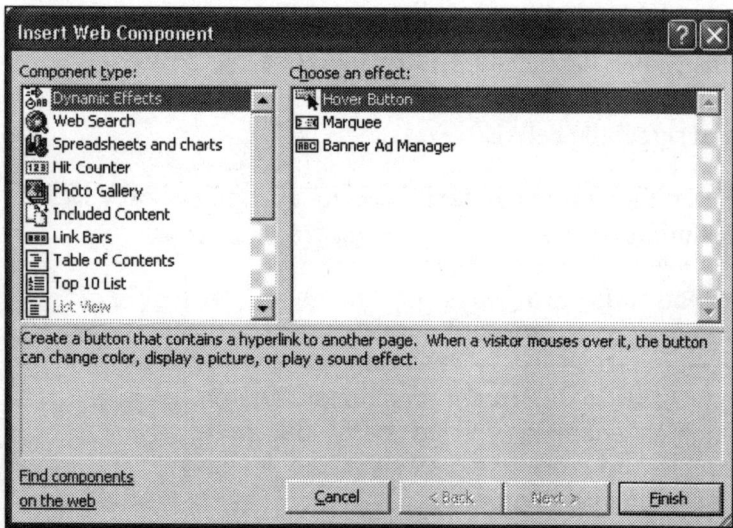

Enter the text (alter the size, font, etc., as you wish, if you want to alter the hover button later, double-click it).

Yahoo

The link is to:

http://www.yahoo.co.uk

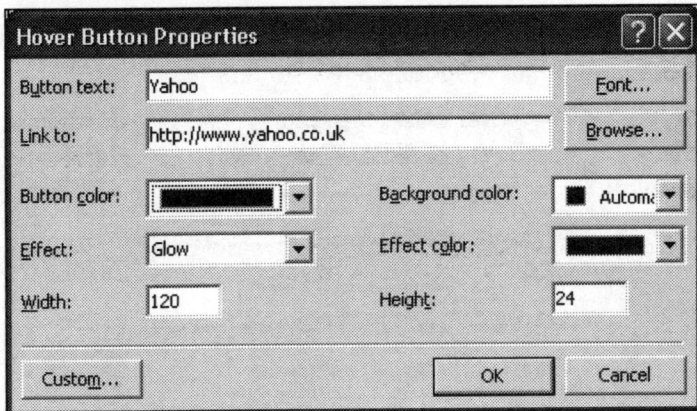

Hover Button Properties

Field	Value	
Button text:	Yahoo	Font...
Link to:	http://www.yahoo.co.uk	Browse...

Button color:	▼	Background color:	■ Autom: ▼
Effect:	Glow ▼	Effect color:	▼
Width:	120	Height:	24

Custom...   OK   Cancel

Do the same for the other cell, this time the text is:

AltaVista

The link is to:

http://www.altavista.com

Enlarge the width of the first column (by clicking and dragging the column divider) so that the second column is just wide enough to accommodate the buttons.

Centre the buttons in each cell.

Save the file and then use the **Preview in Browser** button to look at it, it should look similar to this.

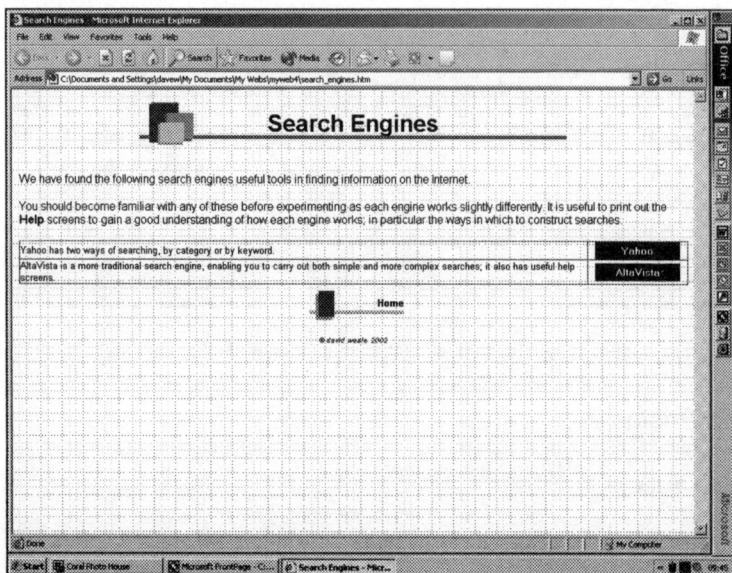

Move the cursor over the hyperlink buttons, if you are using the latest browsers, the buttons should glow (they are hover buttons).

Click the link **Home** and the first page should appear, notice how this also contains navigation buttons.

Click the link (on this page) to **Search Engines** to go back to the second page.

Graphics

Switch back to **FrontPage**.

It is time to insert a graphic image into the page. Position the cursor in the top section of the page, to the right of the title.

Pull down the **Insert** menu, **Picture** and then **Clip Art**. Choose a picture of a computer (by entering the word *Computer* in the **Search text** box).

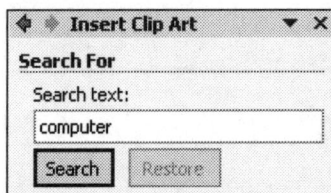

Insert the image and size it (if necessary) by dragging a corner until it fits easily into the section.

Save the file; you will be asked if you want to save the embedded image, answer **OK** (you may want to rename the image file name to something you will remember).

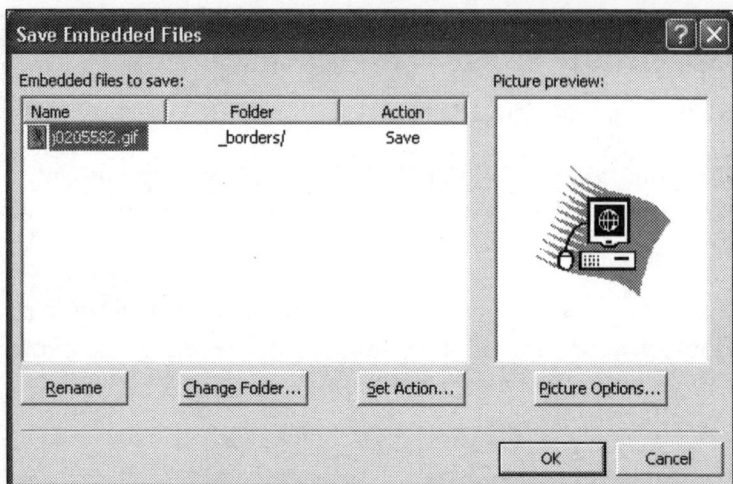

Preview in Browser and you can see how it will look.

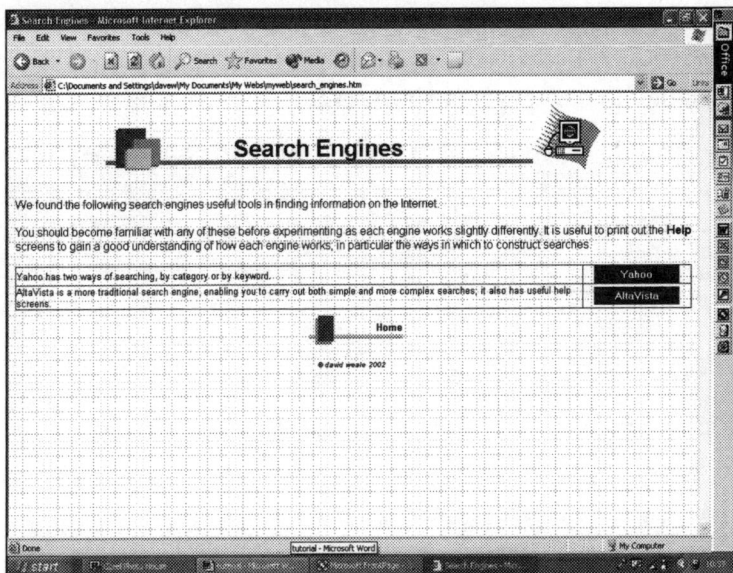

As this image was included in the top section of the page, it will appear on all the pages.

Now to add another page, switch back to the **FrontPage** (check you are in **Navigation View**) and make sure the top page (*Cyrils Cyber Cafe*) is selected.

Click the **New Page** button.

The new page should be on the same level as the page titled **Search Engines** (drag it into position if not) and rename the new page as **Contacts**.

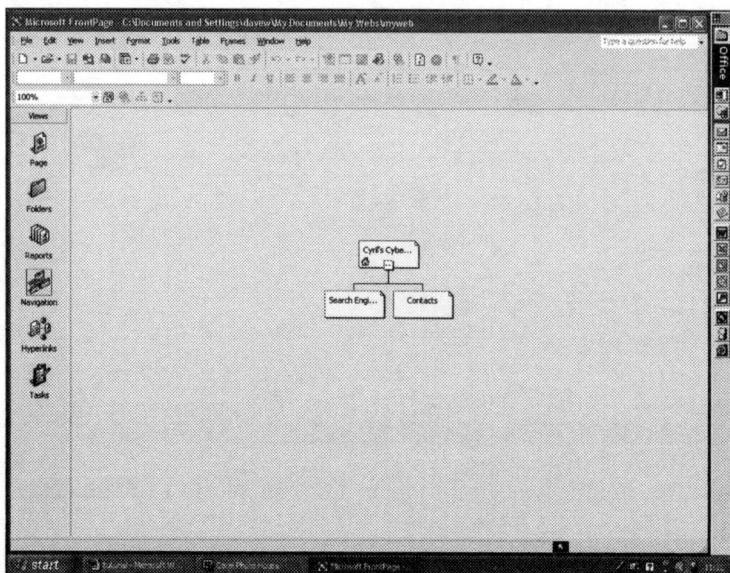

Now double-click the new page and create a space (in the middle section) using the **Return** key.

Add the following table to the middle section of the page using appropriate pictures or motion clips from **Clip Art**.

	Visit us	Upper Street, Yeovil, Somerset.
	Phone us	01935-99796
	Email us	Cyril@Cyrilscafe.demon.co.uk

Adjust the size of the images by right-clicking each and selecting **Picture Properties** from the menu, setting the **Width** at 60 pixels.

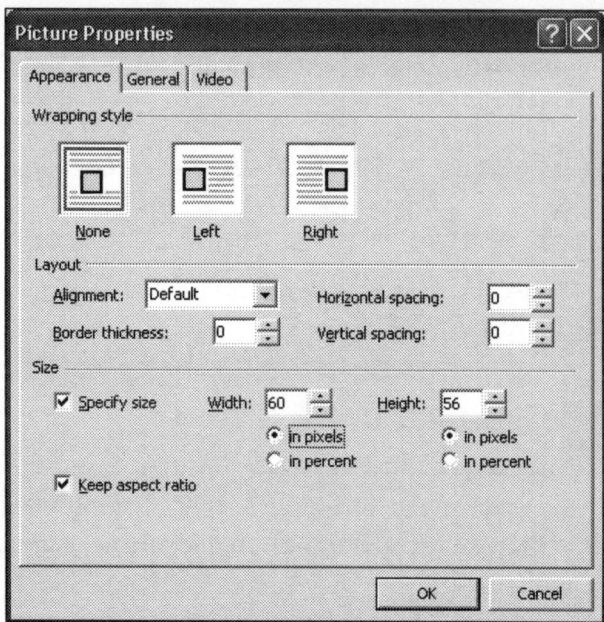

The images should be centred within their cells.

Adjust the column widths to the minimum consistent with the contents.

With the cursor inside the table, pull down the **Table** menu, choosing **Table Properties** and **Table**.

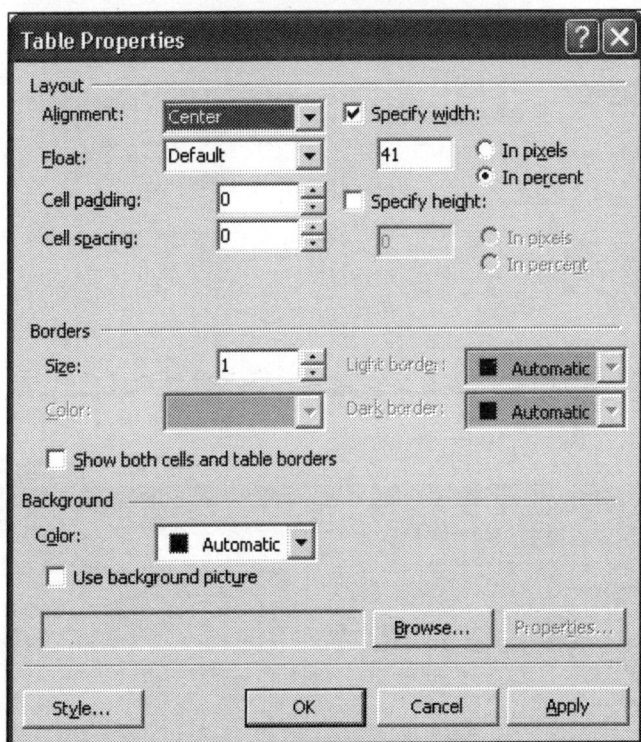

Alter the **Alignment** to **Center** (this centres the table on the page).

Save the page (you may wish to rename the pictures as something meaningful when you save the embedded images).

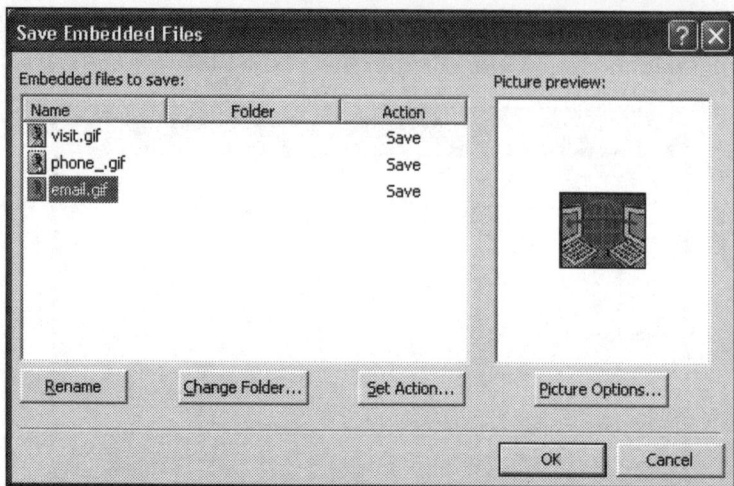

Finally, **Preview** in Browser.

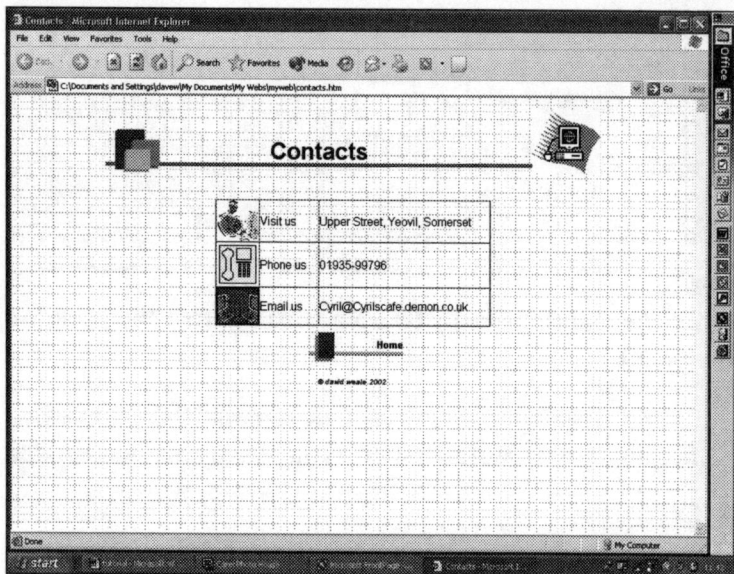

Switch back to **FrontPage**.

Since you have added an email address it would be useful to make this a clickable hyperlink so the viewer could send you an email by clicking on it (this would load their email editor automatically).

Highlight the email address and click the **Hyperlink** button on the toolbar.

You will see the following dialog box.

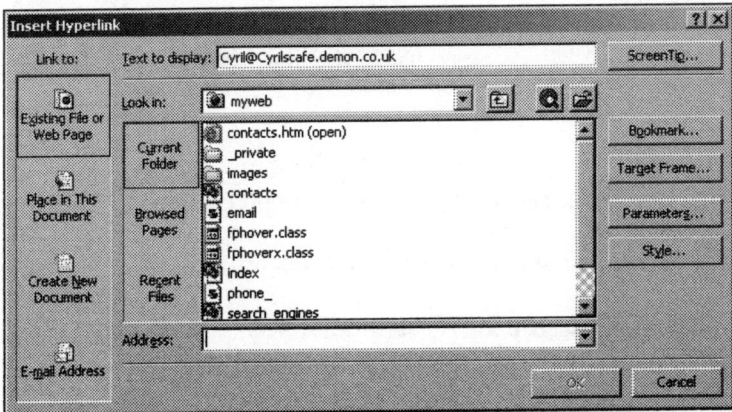

47

Click the **E-mail** button and enter the email address in the box.

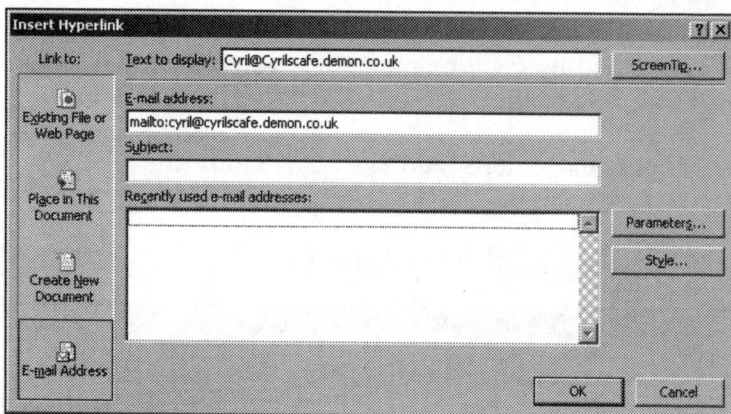

Click **OK** until you get back to the page, you will see that the email address is now underlined and coloured.

Save the page and view it in the browser.

At this stage you have created a web site consisting of three pages, use the navigation buttons along the bottom of the screen to see how far you have progressed.

Switch back to **FrontPage**, make sure you are in **Navigation** view and add a new page. If necessary, drag this page to be on the same level as the other two pages and change the title of the page to:

Interesting Web Sites

You should see a similar screen to that shown below.

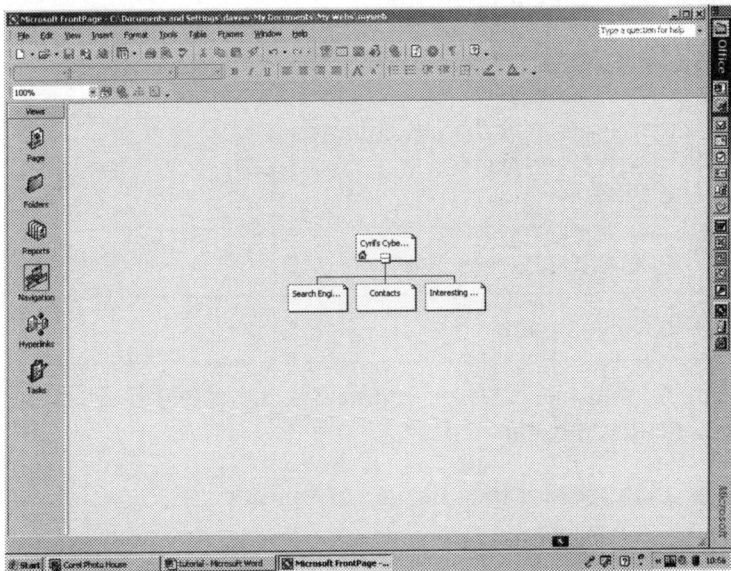

Double-click the new page and add the following text to the middle section of the page (create a space before the text).

For your use we have gathered some web sites that are of interest to us and may be of interest to you.

By going to these pages you are moving outside of our own web site and there are two easy ways to return. Either click the HOME button on the toolbar or use the BACK button (clicking it as many times as necessary to return).

Please colour the words in upper case **red** using the **Font Color** button.

After the text insert this table.

The text appears in the left column.

The BBC	
The Telegraph newspaper	
The X Files page	

You should insert hover buttons for the actual links in the right column of the table.

The addresses for the links are as follows.

http://www.bbc.co.uk

http://www.telegraph.co.uk

http://www.x-files.com

Centre the hover buttons in the cells and adjust the column width of the table to fit the text, finally centring the table.

Save the file, the end result may look similar to this when **Previewed in Browser**.

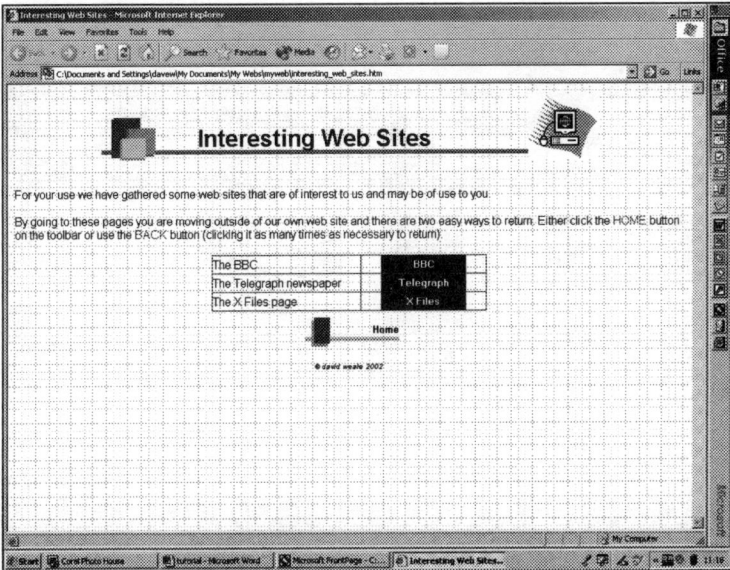

Switch back to **FrontPage** and in **Navigation View**, click the **Interesting Web Sites** page and drag it between the other two pages (on the same level).

This rearranges the pages and they then appear on the navigation bars in the new sequence (which in this instance looks a little tidier).

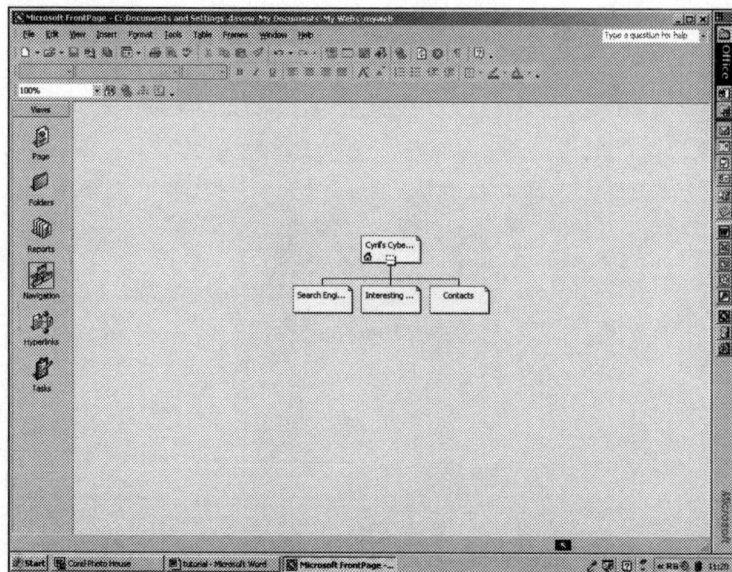

Switch to the browser, click the **Home** hyperlink and you can see along the bottom of the home page, the hyperlinks to all the other pages (on the same level).

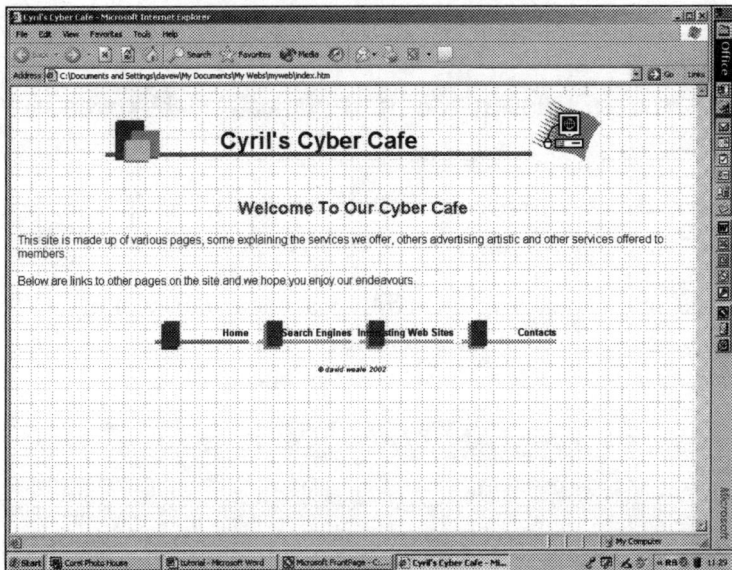

Spelling

Switch back to **FrontPage**.

At this stage it might be advisable to check the spelling of your text (you must **always** do this before publishing your site and it helps to do it periodically while you are working).

Click the spell-checker button on the toolbar, checking and altering your spelling as necessary.

Note that when you are editing a page, the spelling will only be checked on the **current** page. If you check spelling when in **Navigation View**, you can check all pages.

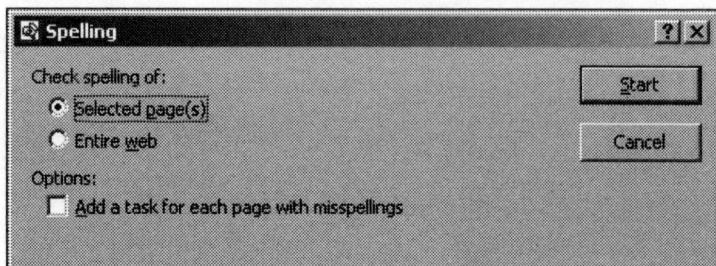

Spelling	? X
Check spelling of:	Start
● Selected page(s)	
○ Entire web	Cancel
Options:	
☐ Add a task for each page with misspellings	

Search forms

In **Navigation** view, add a new page, position it beneath the **Search Engines** page.

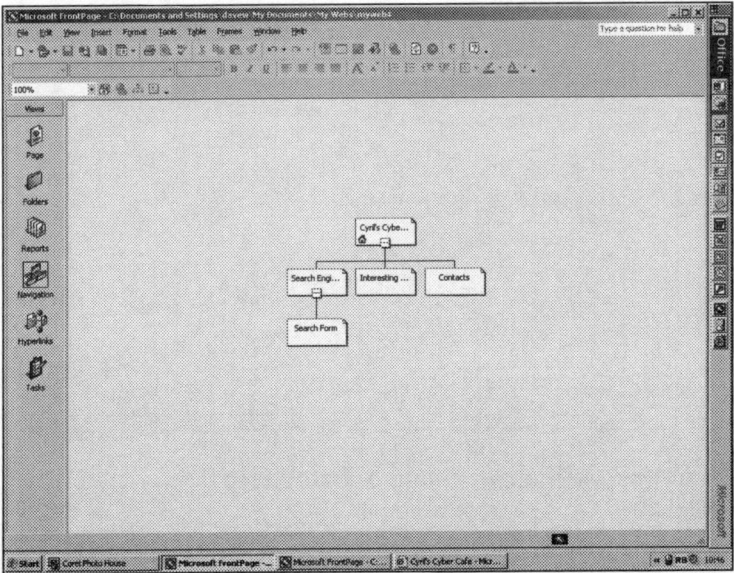

Title it **Search Form** and double-click it to display the page.

Create a space in the middle section of the page and pull down the **Insert** menu, followed by **Web Component** and then **Web Search**.

This will create a search form so that anyone can search your site for words or phrases. Accept the default settings on the screen.

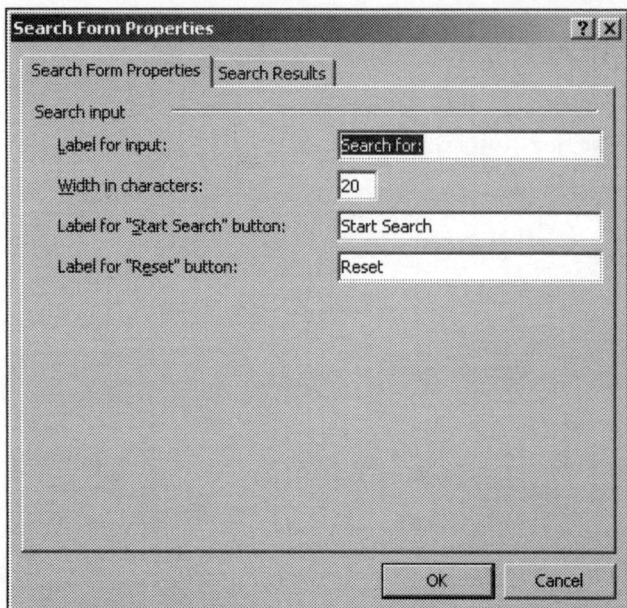

Search Form Properties

Search Form Properties	Search Results

Search input

Label for input:	Search for:
Width in characters:	20
Label for "Start Search" button:	Start Search
Label for "Reset" button:	Reset

OK   Cancel

Your page will now contain a search form.

Save the page.

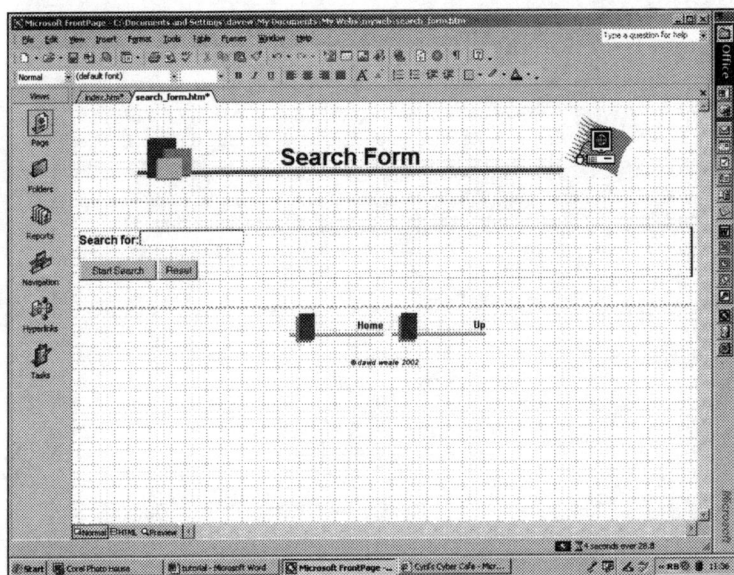

This will not work properly until the site is published to a server that contains the necessary FrontPage extensions.

Marquee

Switch back to **Navigation View** and add a new page, this time positioning it below the **Contacts** page and giving it the title **Staff**.

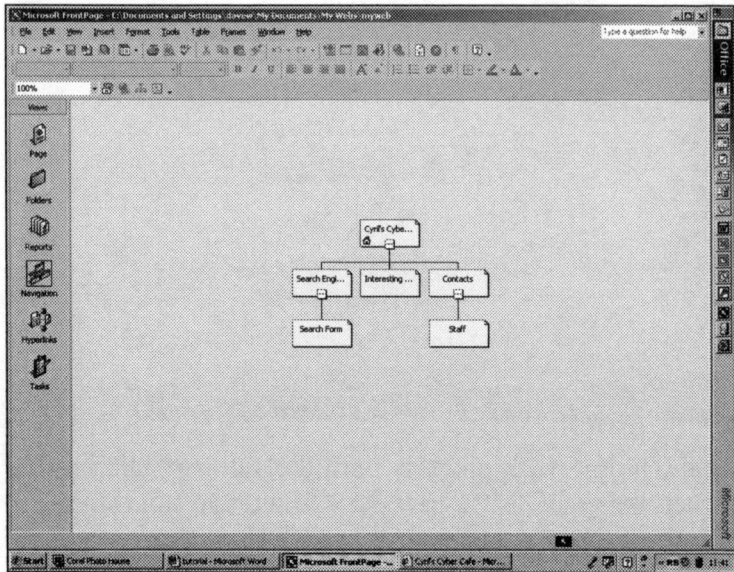

Double-click the page to view it and pull down the **Insert** menu, followed by **Web Component** and **Marquee**.

Add the following text and change the width to 70%, alter the various settings and alter the **Style** settings (**Format**, **Font**, etc.) until you have something reasonable.

This page contains thumbnails of the staff; click any to see a larger picture.

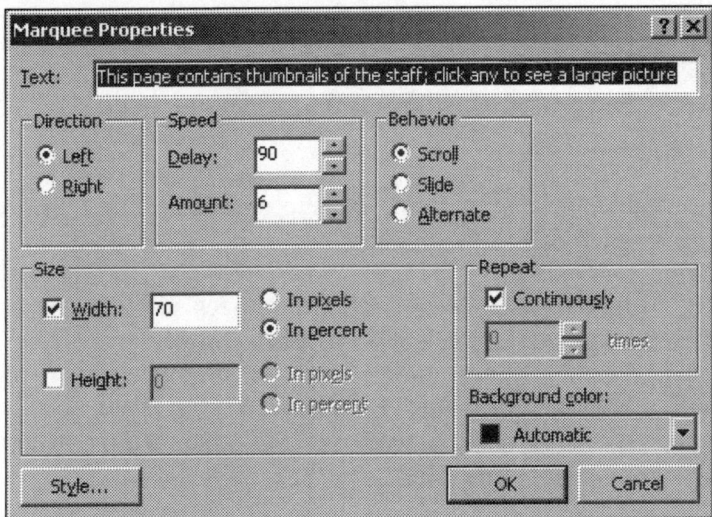

Marquee Properties

Text: `This page contains thumbnails of the staff; click any to see a larger picture`

Direction
- ● Left
- ○ Right

Speed
- Delay: `90`
- Amount: `6`

Behavior
- ● Scroll
- ○ Slide
- ○ Alternate

Size
- ☑ Width: `70`
  - ○ In pixels
  - ● In percent
- ☐ Height: `0`
  - ○ In pixels
  - ○ In percent

Repeat
- ☑ Continuously
  - `0` times

Background color:
- ■ Automatic

Style...   OK   Cancel

Centre the marquee.

You will need to **Preview in Browser** to see how the Marquee actually works.

Thumbnails

Move the cursor below the **Marquee** and create a table (2 columns, 1 row).

Insert a couple of pictures or photographs from **Clipart** (one in each cell of the table).

Right-click each photo (or clipart images if there are no photos installed) and select **Auto Thumbnail**.

This reduces the image to the size you have set for thumbnails (to alter these settings use **Tools**, **Page Options**, **Auto Thumbnail**).

Adjust the column widths as necessary and centre each thumbnail within its cell.

Size the table and centre on the page.

Save the page and then click the **Preview in Browser** button, if you then click on the thumbnail you will see the original image.

To return to your page use the **Back** button and it may be an idea to put some text on the page to explain this, e.g.

After viewing, click the **Back** button to return to the previous page

Horizontal lines

Switch back to **FrontPage** and position the cursor below the **Marquee**, pull down the **Insert** menu and select **Horizontal Line**.

Insert another horizontal line below the table.

Save the page and **Preview in Browser** and you should see something approximating to that shown below.

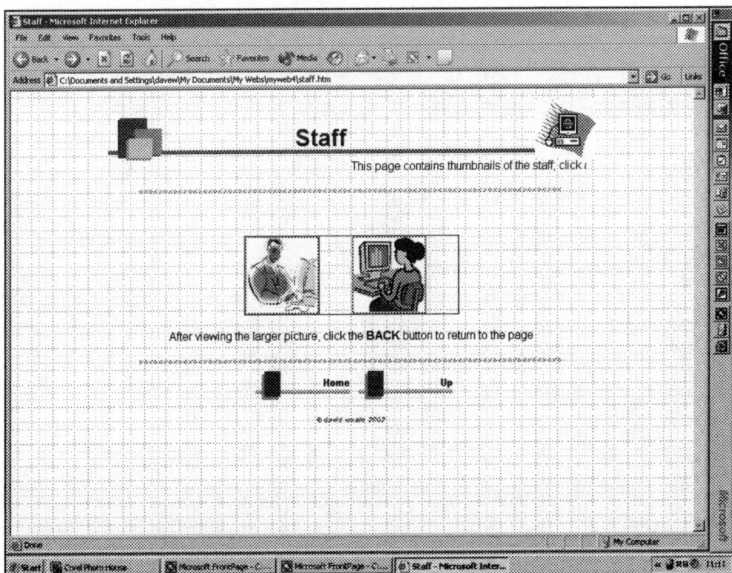

Feedback forms

A very useful tool is being able to create forms that the viewer completes and submits back to you (via your server).

It is important to ensure that the data will be in a form you can easily use and this is something that needs discussion with your ISP (there are programs available that will translate the data into a manageable form).

Using **FrontPage Explorer** (navigation view), create a new page on a level with the other three main pages and call this **Feedback Form**.

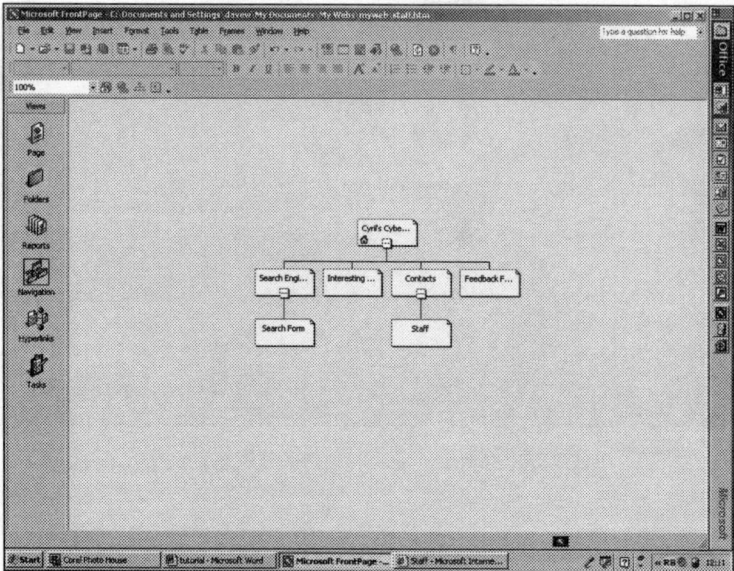

Open this page and position the cursor in the middle section.

Add the following text (**Return**ing after the text).

Please use this form to feedback any comments to us.

Pull down the **Insert** menu, followed by **Form** and **Drop Down Box**.

Double click the data entry box on the left of the form.

Drop-Down Box Properties dialog box:

Name:	D1	

Choice	Selected	Value	
			Add...
			Modify...
			Remove
			Move Up
			Move Down

Height: 1   Allow multiple selections: ○ Yes   ⦿ No

Tab order:

Style...   Validate...   OK   Cancel

You will see this dialog box.

Add the following choices (use the **Add** button to create each).

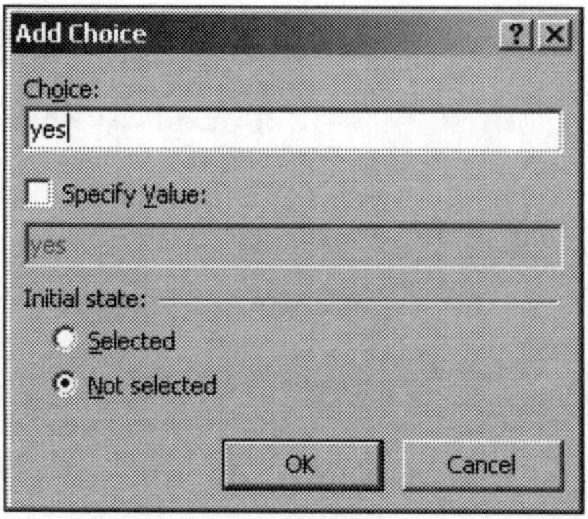

yes

no

do not know

Drop-Down Box Properties   ? ✕

_N_ame: D1

Choice	Selected	Value	
yes	No		Add...
no	No		Modify...
do not know	No		Remove
			Move Up
			Move Down

Height: `1`   Allow multiple selections: ○ _Y_es

Tab order: `      `   ● N_o_

Style...   _V_alidate...   OK   Cancel

Your form should now look like this.

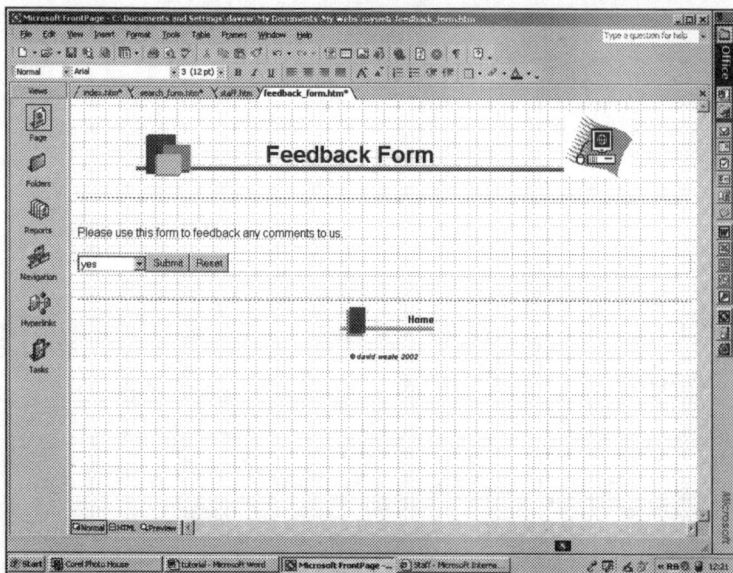

Position the cursor *between* the drop-down box and the **Submit** button and **Return** to move the **Submit** and **Reset** buttons down.

Position the cursor to the left of the drop-down box and type the following text.

Have you visited our site before?

Highlight the text *and* the drop-down box and pull down the **Insert** menu, then **Form** and **Label**.

Your form should now look like this.

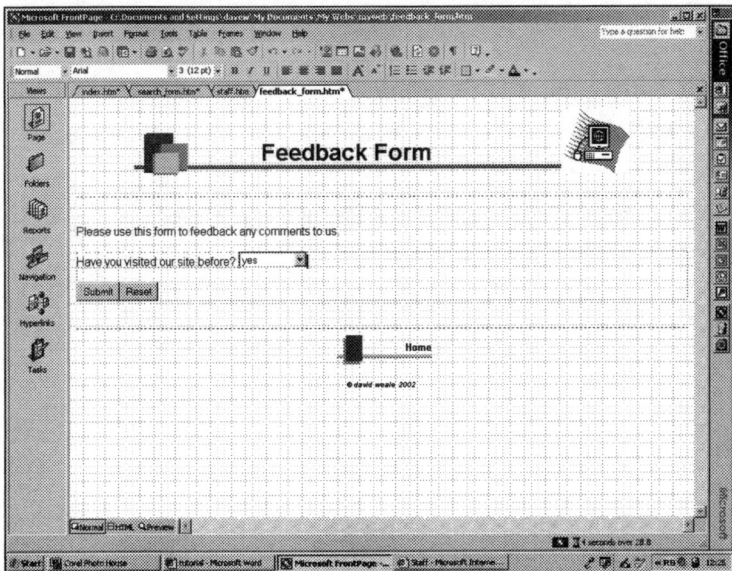

Add another **Drop-Down Menu** (below the first one) containing the following choices.

Excellent

Needs some changes

Create a **label**, the text is:

What do you think of our site?

Finally insert a **Text Area** beneath this question (**Insert, Form**).

Create a **label** with the following text.

Specify any changes you would make to our site

The form should resemble this when **Previewed in Browser** (after you have resized the boxes as necessary and centred the **Submit** and **Reset** buttons).

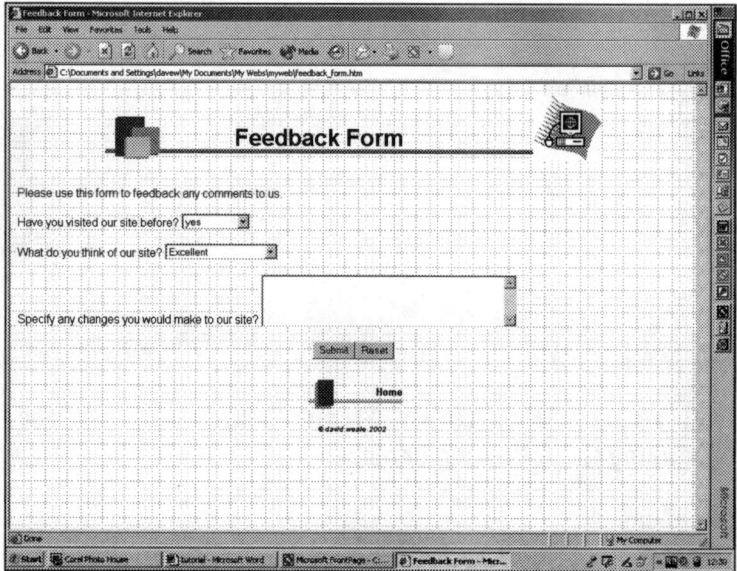

Practice

Now to get some practice, please create two new pages, the first called **About Us** (which should be positioned on the same level as the other main pages).

The second page is to be called **Coffee** and should be positioned underneath the page called **About Us**.

The final structure should be like this.

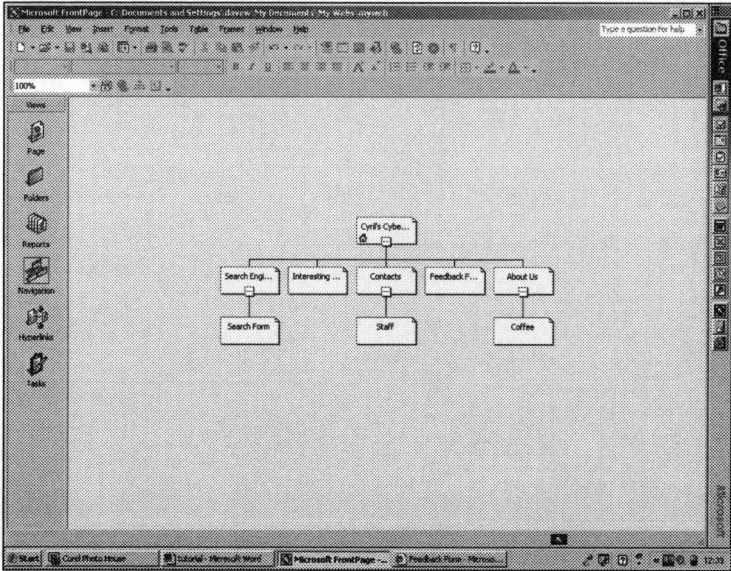

The content of **About Us** should contain the following text (there should be a space before and after the text).

We are a cyber cafe supporting the following activities:

A coffee bar

An outlet for artists

A second hand record stall

Internet access

Highlight the last four lines and pull down the **Format** menu, followed by **Bullets and Numbering**.

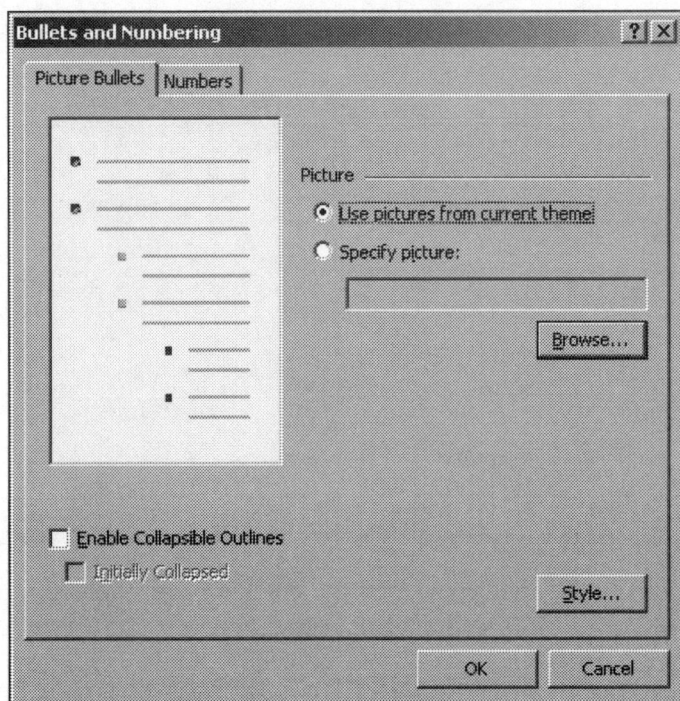

Select **Use pictures from current theme**.

The page should look like this (in the browser).

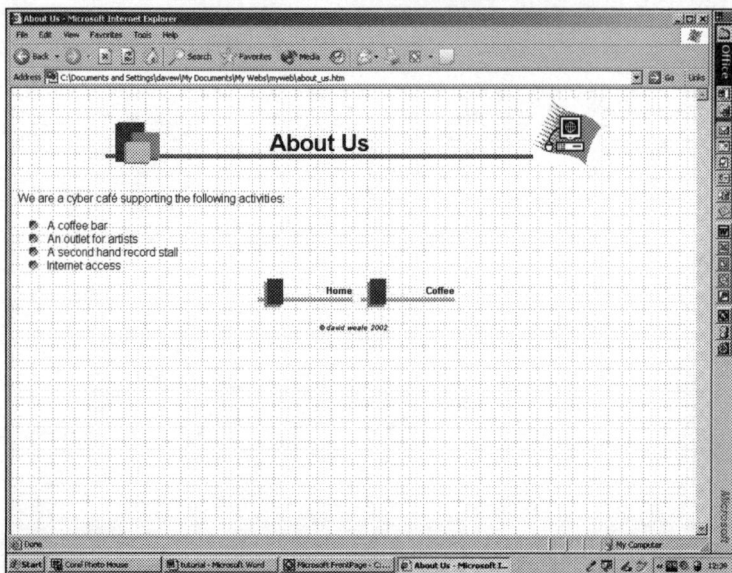

Enter the following text into the **Coffee** page (there should be a space before and after the text).

Indulge yourself in some of the best cups of coffee and cakes available in town. We use a Spanish espresso coffee machine and sell home made cakes.

Then insert a picture (from **Clip Art**) of a cake and centre the picture, then create a space below it.

The page could look like this (in the browser), when you have finished.

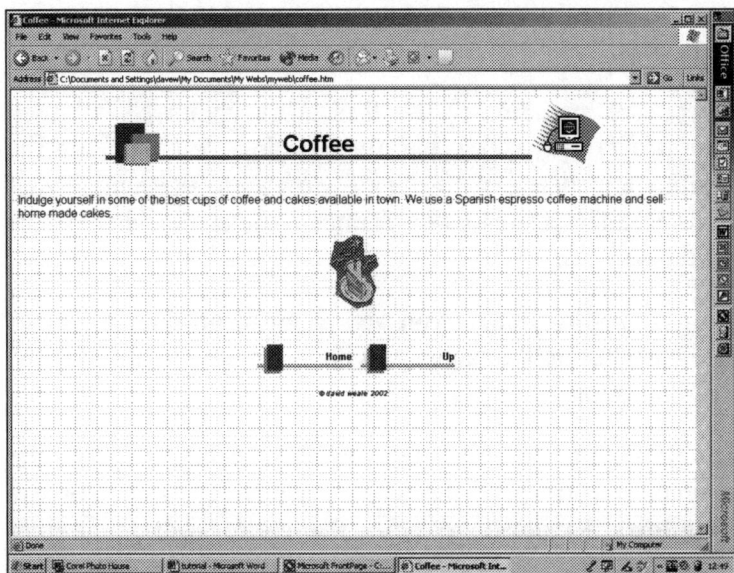

You have now finished the web site. Look at the site you have created in its entirety to see what you have achieved.

Close all the open pages (**File, Close**).

Frames

The final part of this course is concerned with the creation of frames.

If you are intending to use frames on your web site then you **must** decide this before planning your site, as the relationship between the pages and their size and layout may be different (as using frames reduces the visible area on the screen).

To get used to frames you are going to produce a frames site based upon the pages you have already created for the original tutorial.

If you want to retain the tutorial files, create a copy of the original site (publish the web to a different folder or use **Windows Explorer** to *copy* the entire web to another location).

Use the **Folder List** button to view the list of files. View the **Folders** and change the name of the **Index.htm** file to **Initial.htm**, ignore the error message that appears but do agree to repair the hyperlinks.

Change the title to Welcome (right-click and then choose **Properties**).

In **Navigation** view delete all the pages from all navigation bars by clicking on the top page (*Welcome*) and then use the **Delete** key.

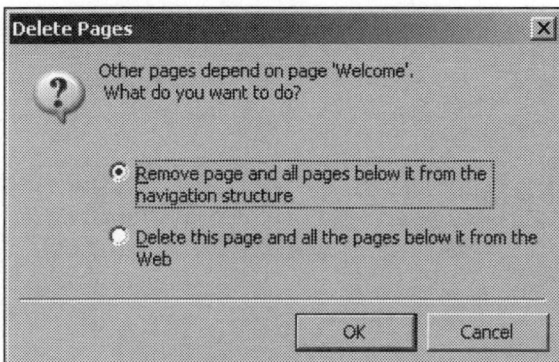

Delete Pages

Other pages depend on page 'Welcome'.
What do you want to do?

○ Remove page and all pages below it from the navigation structure

○ Delete this page and all the pages below it from the Web

[OK] [Cancel]

Pull down the **File** menu, followed by **New**, **Page or Web**, **Page Templates**, **Frames Pages**), finally selecting the **Contents** page.

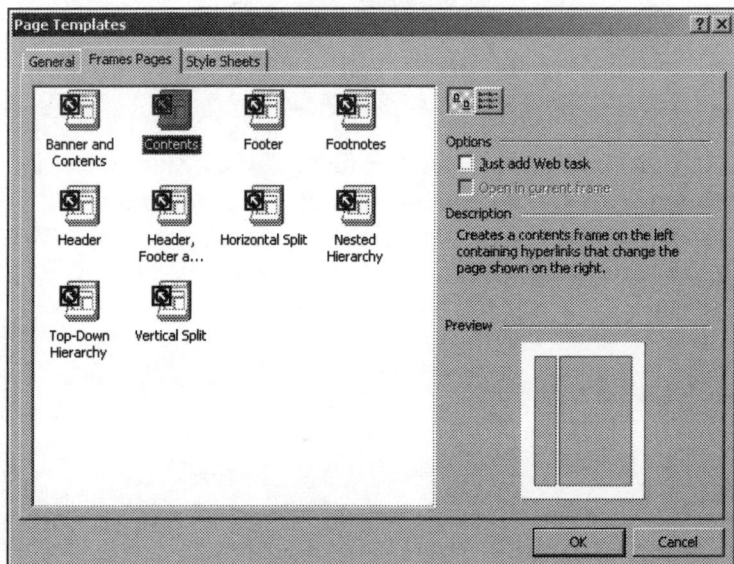

Page Templates

General | Frames Pages | Style Sheets

Banner and Contents
Contents
Footer
Footnotes
Header
Header, Footer a...
Horizontal Split
Nested Hierarchy
Top-Down Hierarchy
Vertical Split

Options
☐ Just add Web task
☐ Open in current frame

Description
Creates a contents frame on the left containing hyperlinks that change the page shown on the right.

Preview

[OK] [Cancel]

You should now see the following screen.

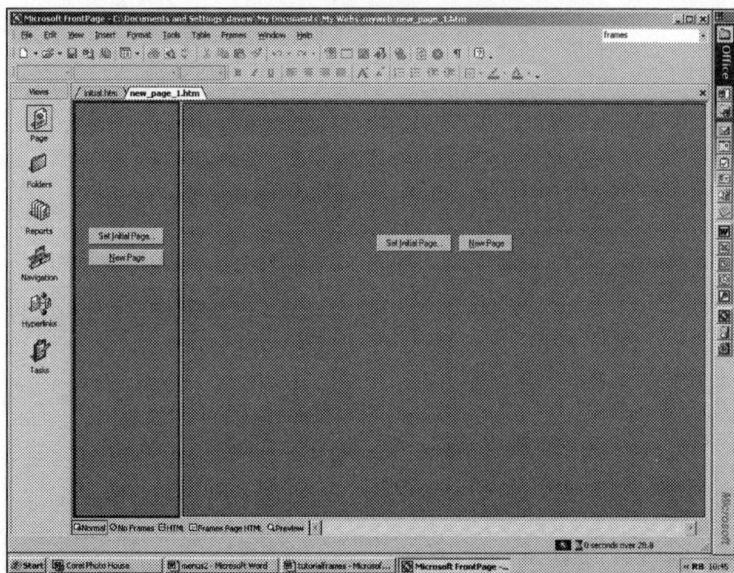

Save the page, giving it the name **Index**, also click the **Change title** button and alter the title to **Home Page**.

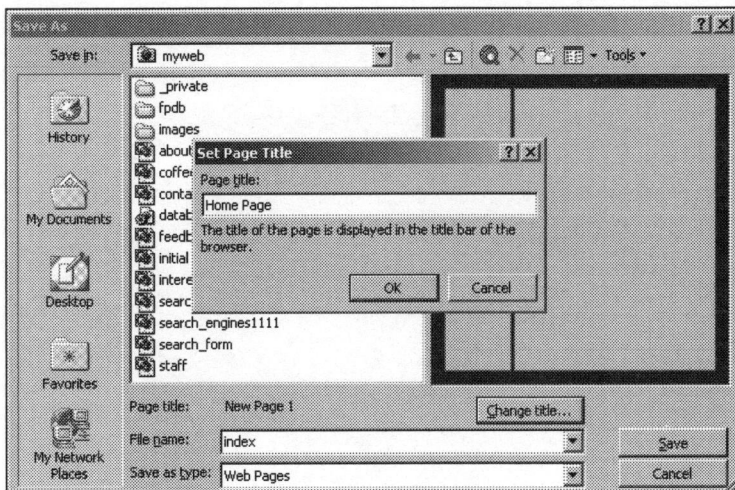

Close all the open pages (**File**, **Close**).

Now to create a new blank page to contain the links to each page within the web (**File**, **New**, **Page or Web**, **New**, **Blank Page**).

Pull down the **Format** menu and choose **Shared Borders**.

For the **Current page** only, choose the option shown below.

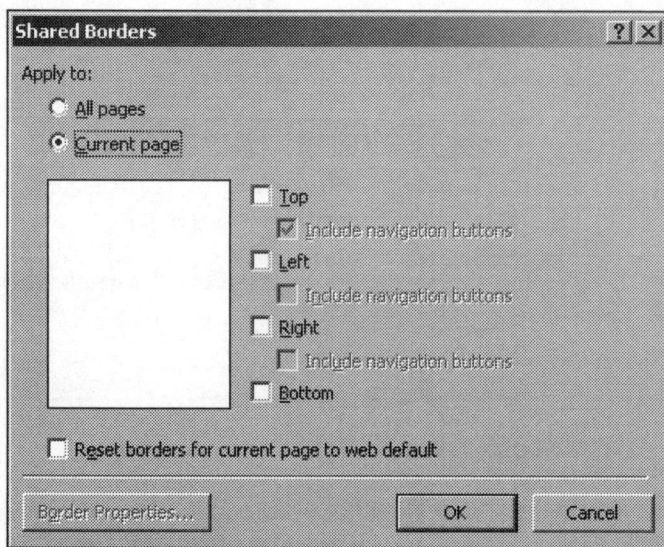

Now, to insert navigation bars, pull down the **Insert** menu followed by **Navigation**.

Select the option **Bar based on navigation structure** and
accept the default settings for the remaining screens.

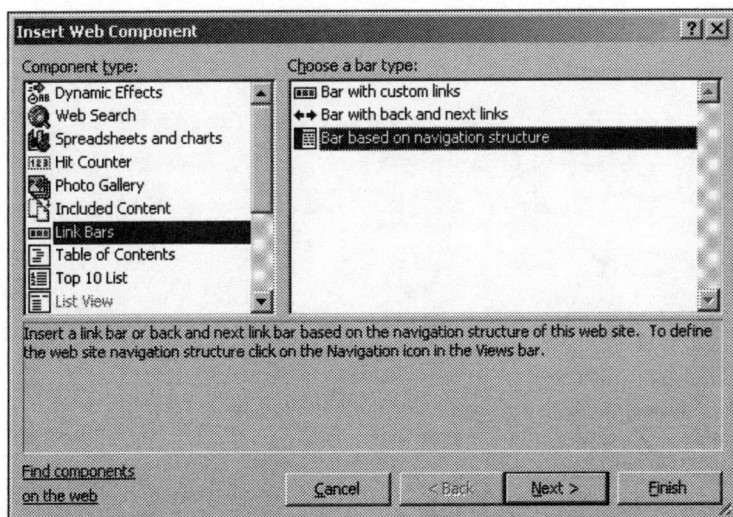

79

Insert a **Navigation Bar** (**Style** - *Vertical*) with links to the **Child** pages.

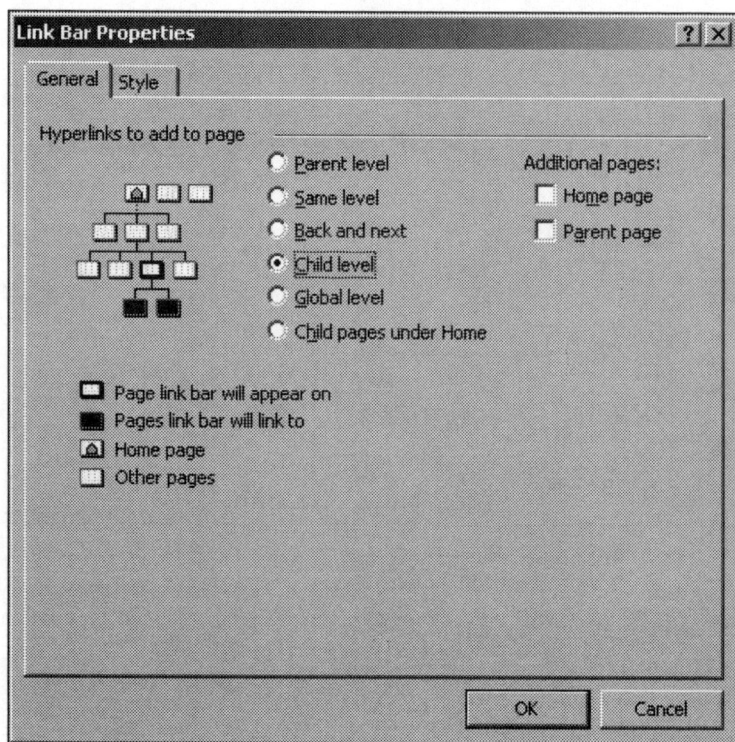

```
Link Bar Properties                                    ? X

 General | Style |

 Hyperlinks to add to page

                        C  Parent level          Additional pages:
   [🏠][⬜][⬜]          C  Same level             ☐ Home page
   [⬜][⬜][⬜]          C  Back and next          ☐ Parent page
   [⬜][⬜][⬜][⬜]       ⊙  Child level
      [⬛][⬛]           C  Global level
                        C  Child pages under Home

   ⬜  Page link bar will appear on
   ⬛  Pages link bar will link to
   🏠  Home page
   ⬜  Other pages

                                          OK        Cancel
```

Save this page (**File, Save As**) as **Links.htm** with the same title (*Links*).

Go to **Navigation view** and click the **Folder List** button on the toolbar (if the **Folder List** is not shown).

Drag the file **Links.htm** underneath the **Home Page** so the screen looks like this.

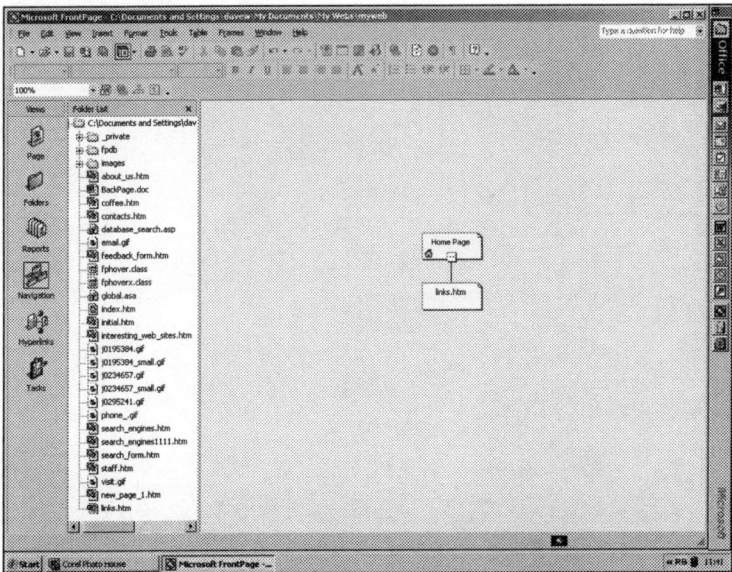

Drag the other pages (*About_us, Coffee, Feedback Form, Staff, Search Engines, Interesting Web Sites* and *Contacts*) **from** the left onto the navigation, underneath the **Links** page.

The final result should look like this.

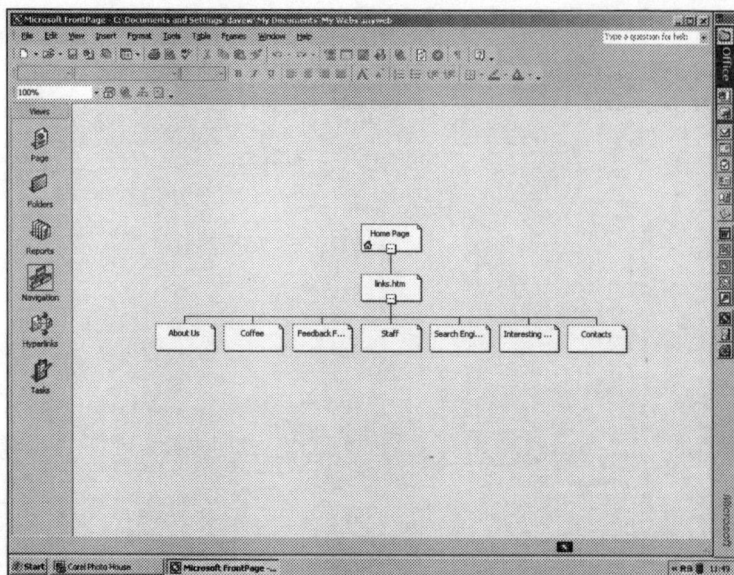

Double-click any of the pages on the bottom level and remove the navigation bars.

Save the page.

Open the page **Index.htm** (*home page*) and **Set** (*left*) **initial page** as **Links.htm**.

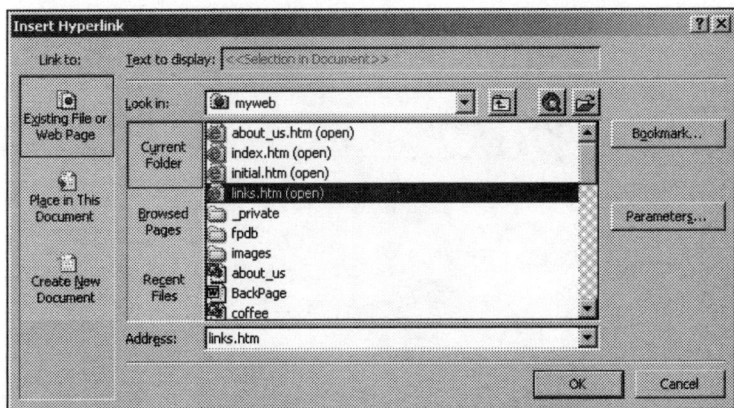

Set the (*right*) **initial page** as **About_us.htm** (*Welcome*).

Move the divider between the frames to show all the links in the left frame.

Save the page.

Close down the web, saving any pages as prompted and open it in the browser (use the **File**, **Open** and **Browse** to locate *Index.htm*).

You should see something like this, with the links on the left and the contents appearing on the right.

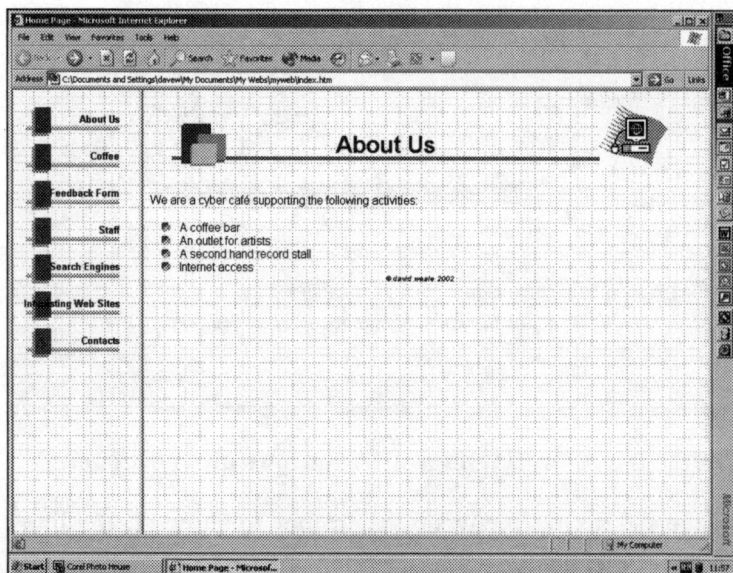

If the frames do not work properly in the browser e.g. the target frame appears on the left replacing the menu, but work in FrontPage, remove and replace the navigation bar.

The Pull-Down Menus

These are explained in sequence, where there is a toolbar button that can be used as a quicker alternative, it is shown on the right of the narrative.

File

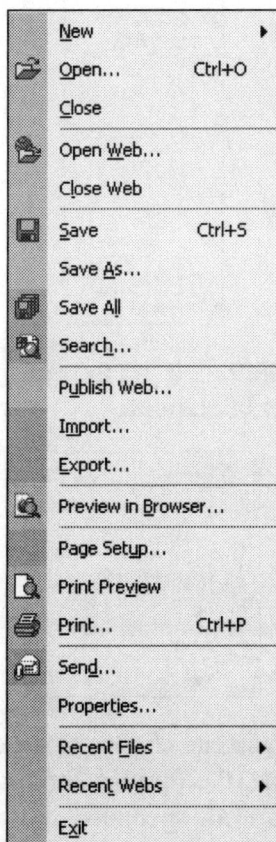

New

When you select this you will be given several choices.

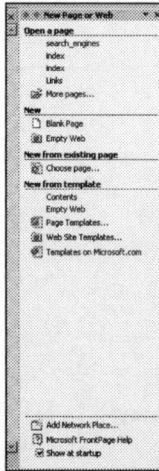

Alternatively, the button on the toolbar gives a slightly different set of choices.

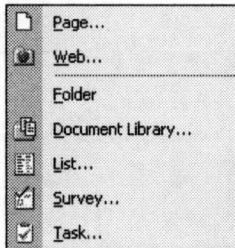

With either menu, you can choose to create a **Page**, a **Web**, a **Folder** or a **Task** (the options for **Document Library**, **List** and **Survey** are all specialist options only available from the Microsoft web site).

However, not all the options will be available; it depends on what **View** you are using, for example the **Folder** option only becomes available within certain views.

Page

You will be given the choice of a **General** page (shown below), **Frames Pages** or **Style Sheets**.

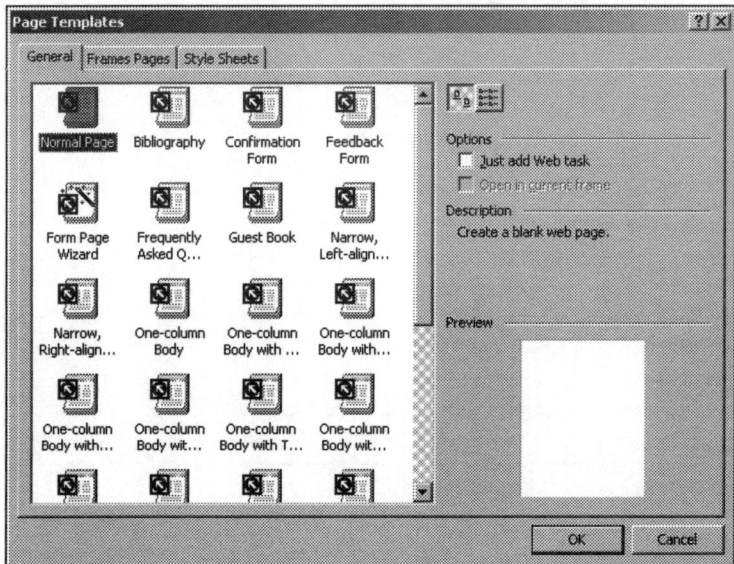

Web

You can choose from a variety of wizards (or choose to begin an empty web), you also need to specify where the web is to be saved.

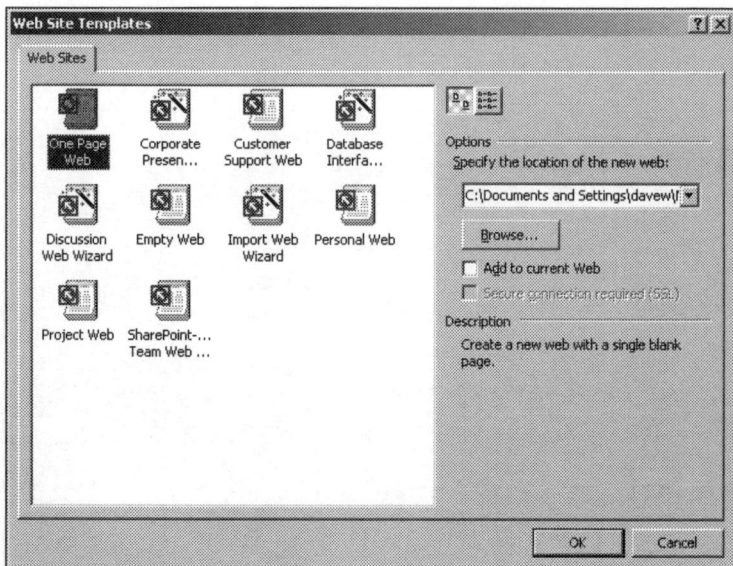

Folder

You can create a new folder (but only when you using certain views, e.g. **Folder** view).

Task

You can add a new task to the web (to remind you to do it) or assign the task to another person.

Open / Open Web

You can either open a page or a complete web using this option (alternatively use the toolbar button).

You can open pages in the current web or within another web.

Close / Close Web

Closes the page or web.

Save / Save As

You can save pages using these commands (remember **Save As** always brings up the dialog box allowing you to make changes).

Save (button shown opposite) saves with whatever settings you chose when you first saved the page/file.

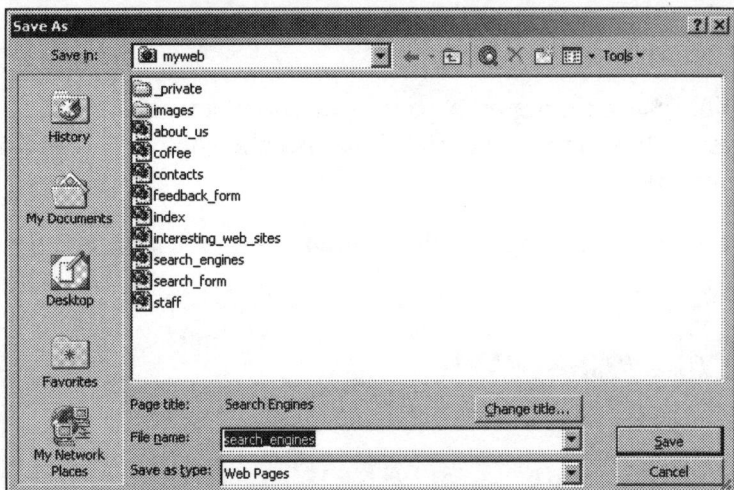

There is an option within the **Save As** screen to alter the
Page title of the page as well as the **File name**.

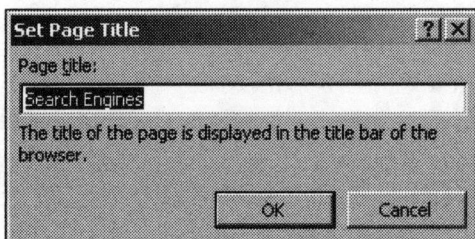

You can save as a template by pulling down the **Save as
type** list.

This means you can set up a page with the theme, borders,
navigation bars and so on and then save it as a template.

The template then appears in the list of layouts that appears
when you create a new page (**File**, **New**).

Search

This is the standard Office search tool (on right of screen) which enables a text search to be made (which can be customised by selecting from the various options or by using the **Advanced Search** (bottom of task pane).

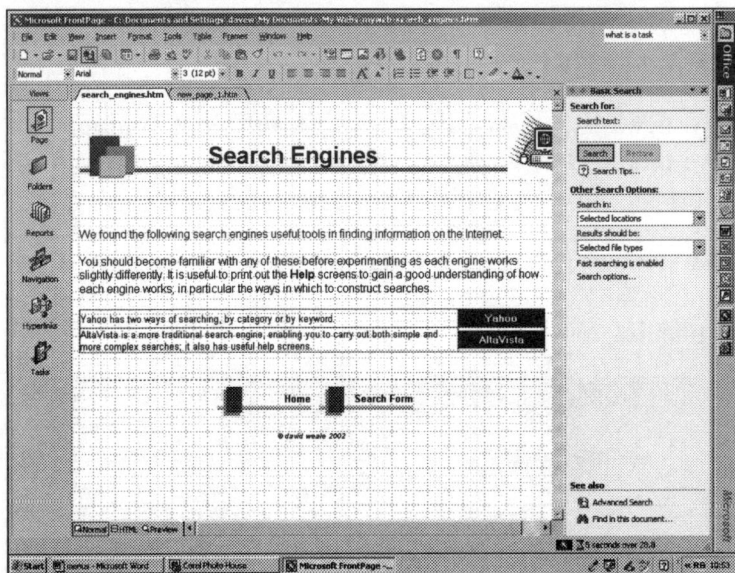

Publish Web

A quick way of publishing your web site to an Intranet, to the Internet or to a disc.

It is *very* important to understand that to copy the entire web it is necessary to **Publish** it as it is otherwise difficult to ensure that all the files making up the web are copied to the new location.

If you want to move the web to a different computer or save it on CD or send it to your ISP, then you must publish it.

You will see a dialog box that allows you to choose where to publish. You need to enter the address of the site you are publishing to.

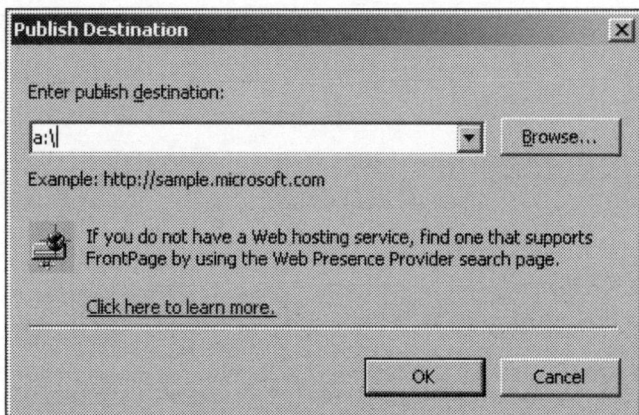

The Program collects the files and you can also select the **Include subwebs**; this will publish any webs that are linked to the present web.

If you have already published or uploaded the web site then you have just publishing the *changed pages* (by clicking the **Options** button).

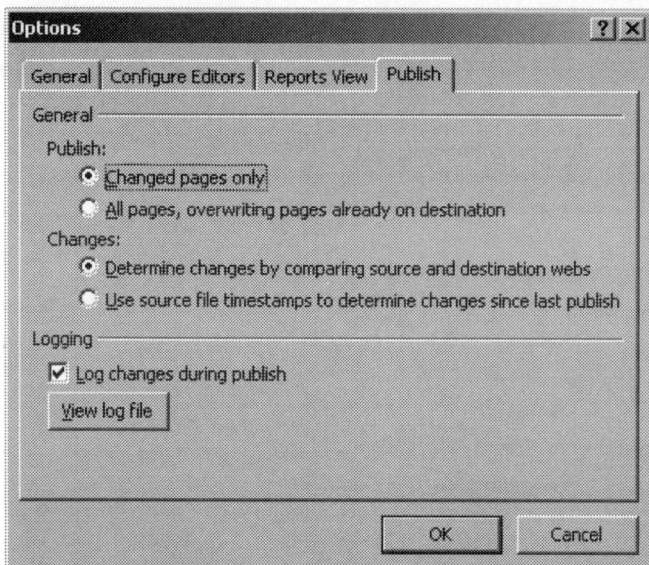

A warning message may appear, normally continue bearing in mind that the warning states that the identified pages may not display properly unless the conditions are met.

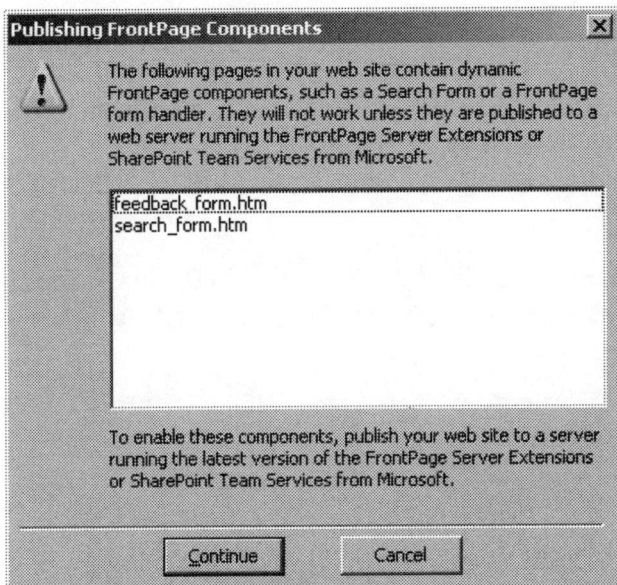

Publishing FrontPage Components

⚠ The following pages in your web site contain dynamic FrontPage components, such as a Search Form or a FrontPage form handler. They will not work unless they are published to a web server running the FrontPage Server Extensions or SharePoint Team Services from Microsoft.

feedback_form.htm
search_form.htm

To enable these components, publish your web site to a server running the latest version of the FrontPage Server Extensions or SharePoint Team Services from Microsoft.

[Continue]   [Cancel]

Finally, a message will appear and you can look at your web in your Internet browser.

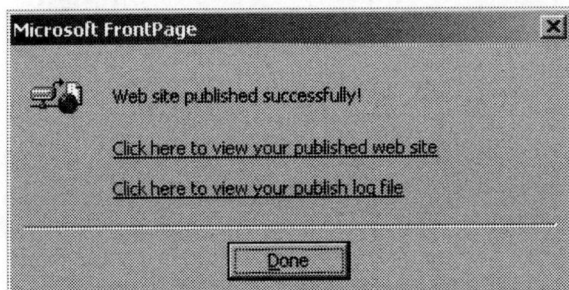

Microsoft FrontPage

Web site published successfully!

Click here to view your published web site

Click here to view your publish log file

[Done]

Import

You can import a file, a folder or a web from your hard disc, an Intranet or the Internet.

File

If you import a file it will be added to the list of files in the current web and you then drag it from the list into the **Navigation** view.

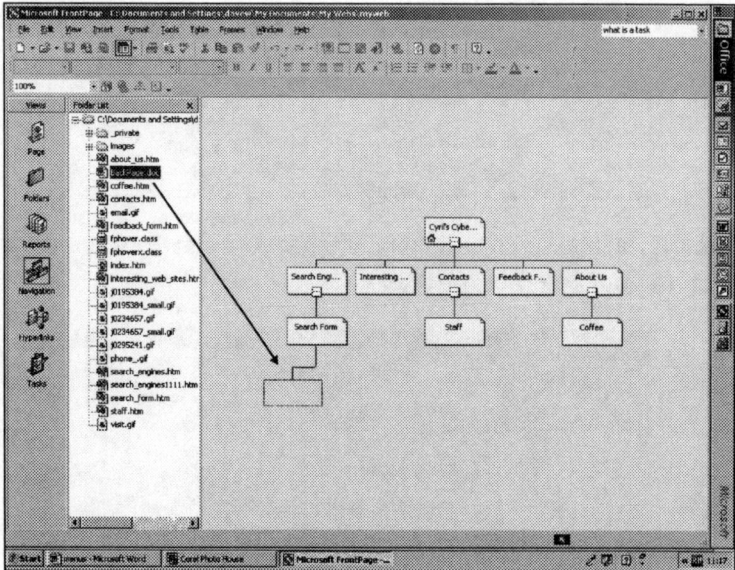

Folder

This imports the contents of a folder (as opposed to a single file) into your current web.

96

Web

You can begin a new web by importing an existing one from the Internet, Intranet or from your hard discs.

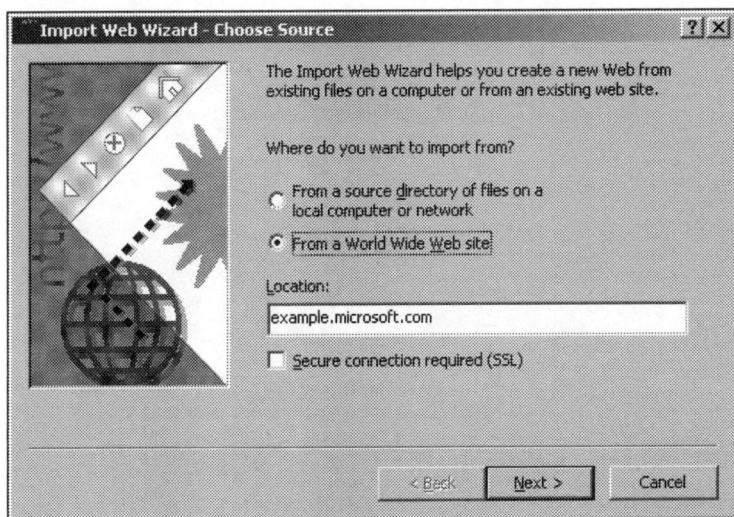

Export

Pages can be exported to another location using this option.

Preview in Browser

The menu command lets you select the browser (if you have installed more than one).

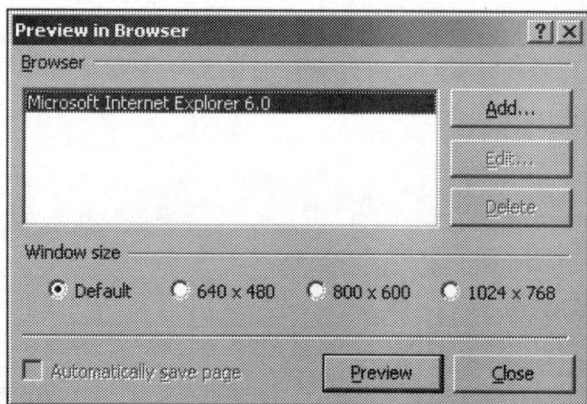

The button just loads the current page in the default browser. Using the button does not give the options shown in the dialog box.

Page Setup

Use this to set margins, headers and footers for printing the page, the settings do not appear on the actual web, just on your printed copy.

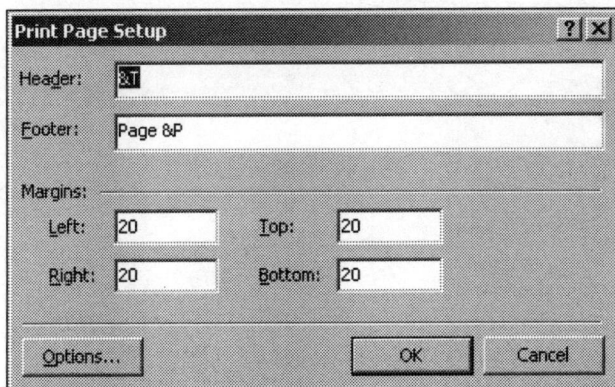

The **Options** button loads the **Print Setup** screen, which is the standard Windows one.

Print Preview

You can preview the pages or the **Navigation View** before actually printing them.

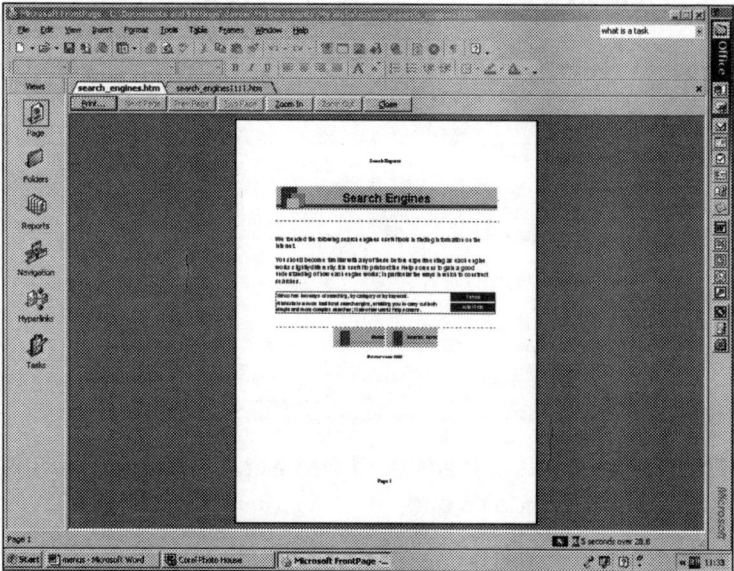

Note the headers and footers (these can be altered in the **Page Setup** option).

Print

The normal print dialog box appears here.

Send

This sends a copy of the current page to an email address. Useful if you are working with others on the web site or want to let others look at pages before they are published.

You can add other pages or files as attachments.

Properties

You can alter various properties of your pages, for example the top and bottom margins.

Exit

Closes the program (you will be prompted to save any pages that have altered since the last save).

Edit

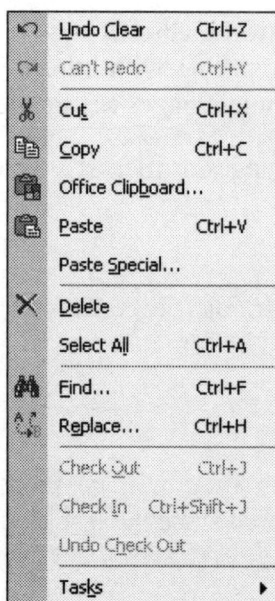

Undo / Redo

You can undo or redo (most) previous actions.

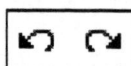

Cut / Copy / Paste

Standard buttons, these function as you would expect.

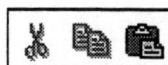

Paste Special

If this command is available (it only works with text), it will give you several options to paste the text. Each may look different depending upon the formatting of the original.

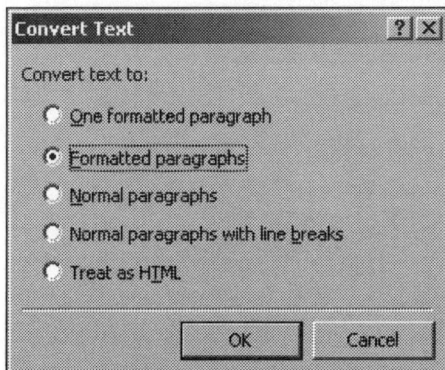

Delete

This deletes the selected files or page (depending upon which view you are in).

Select All

This selects all the items in the body section of the current page (so you can cut or copy them).

Find / Replace

These operate in a similar way to a word processor; they find a word or phrase (and replace it with another if you have chosen this option).

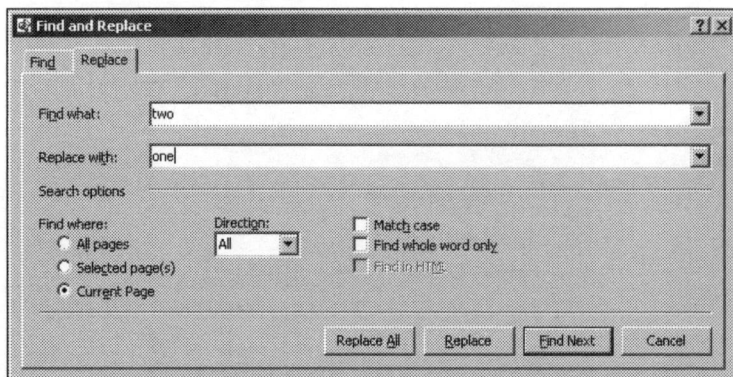

Check Out / Check In

Let you look at a page created by someone else but not alter it.

Tasks

You can add a task to the list of tasks (linked to the current web) so you can be reminded to do the task or you can assign the task to someone else.

By clicking on the **Tasks** button in the **View** bar, you can do things to the task, e.g. start it (this will load the page associated with the task).

View

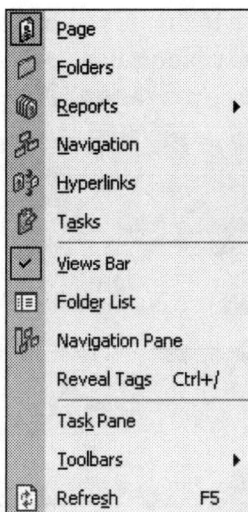

Page (to) Tasks

These are alternatives to the buttons on the left-hand side of the screen. This could be useful if for example you have hidden the buttons (by dragging the side of the window to give more space to the main screen or by turning off the **Views Bar**).

Views Bar

This commands turns on or off the **Views Bar**.

Folder List / Navigation Pane

These display or hide the lists, you can also use the toolbar button which also enables the **Folder List** or the **Navigation Pane** to be displayed

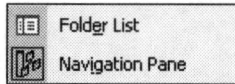

The illustration shows the **Navigation Pane**.

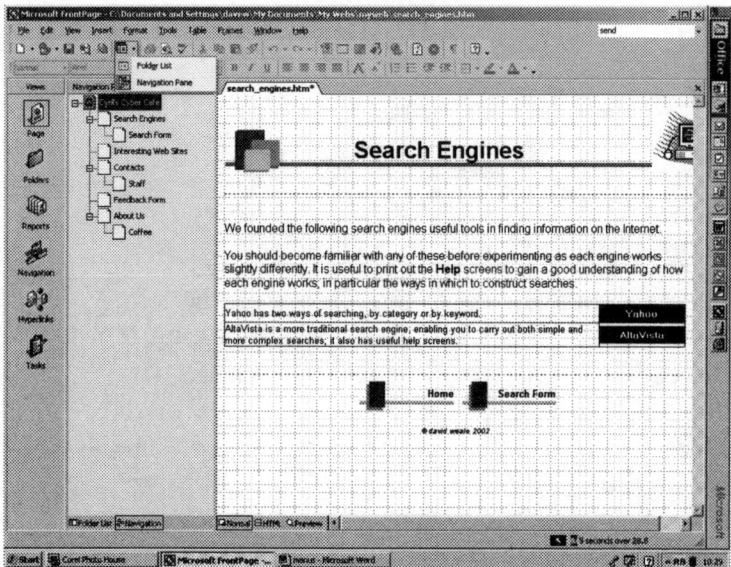

Reveal tags

This displays the **html** tags around text, pictures, etc., within the web pages.

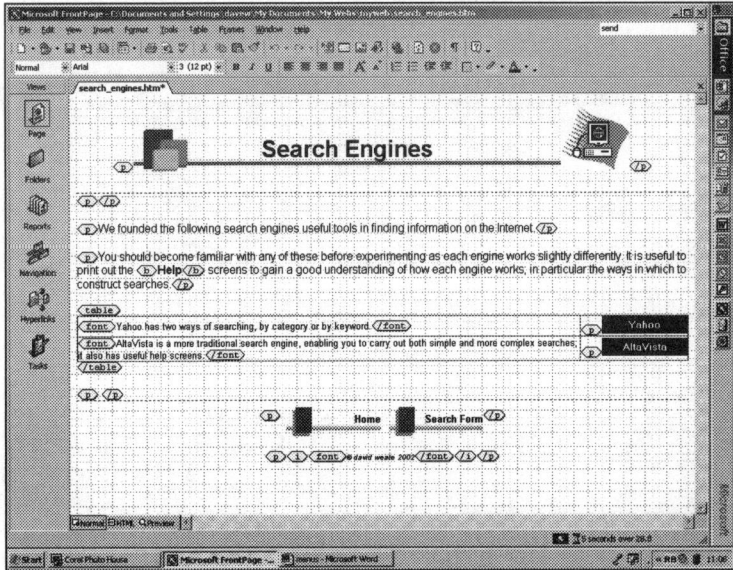

Task Pane

The **Task Pane** can be displayed on the right of the screen, this details the various activities that can be carried out (the contents of the pane alter as different screens are displayed).

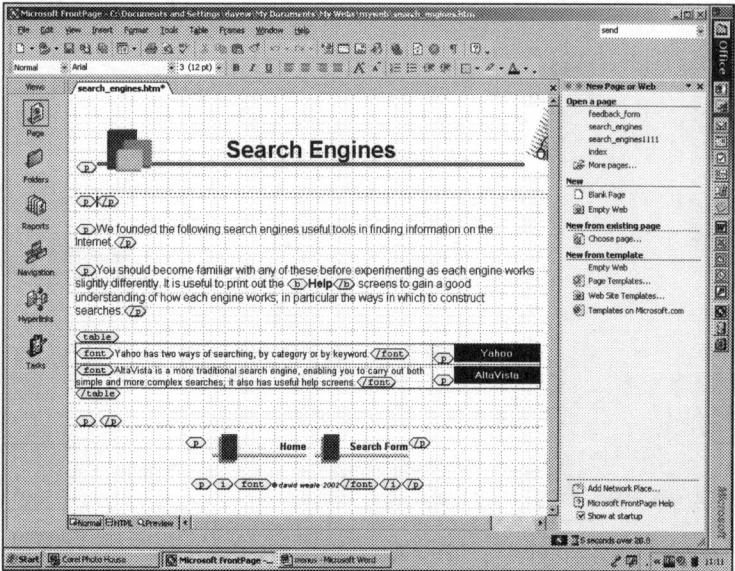

Toolbars

This command displays toolbars, if you use a command regularly then it is easier and quicker to use a toolbar button than the pull-down menus.

A tick to the right of the toolbar name shows that the toolbar is displayed, to hide a toolbar, click on the name to remove the tick.

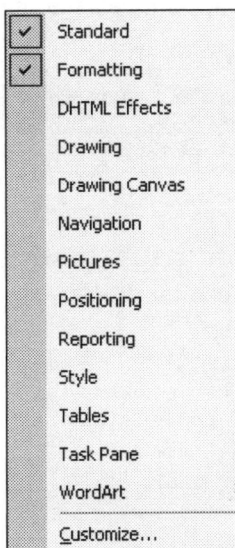

✓	Standard
✓	Formatting
	DHTML Effects
	Drawing
	Drawing Canvas
	Navigation
	Pictures
	Positioning
	Reporting
	Style
	Tables
	Task Pane
	WordArt
	Customize...

Standard / Formatting Toolbars

These are normally displayed by default.

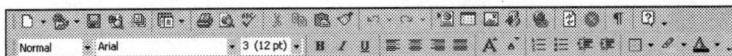

You can choose to display these toolbars on one or two rows by clicking the button to the right of the **Help** button.

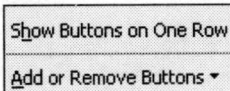

Show Buttons on One Row

Add or Remove Buttons ▾

Pictures Toolbar

This contains the tools to manipulate pictures and other graphics and should appear automatically when you select an image.

Refresh

Refreshes the page to reflect any changes you have made, you can use the **F5** key or the toolbar button shown opposite.

Insert

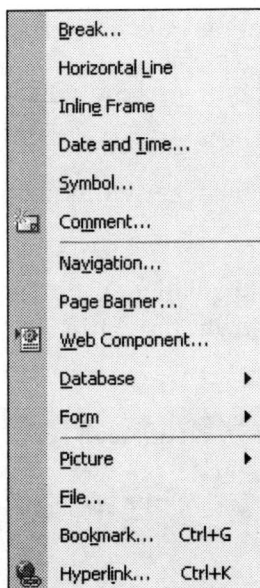

Break

Inserts a line break at the cursor position.

You are given a choice of how you want the line break formatted.

The line break command gives more control than simply using the **Return** key.

If you want to create smaller space than with the **Return** key, try holding down the **Shift** key while using the **Return** key.

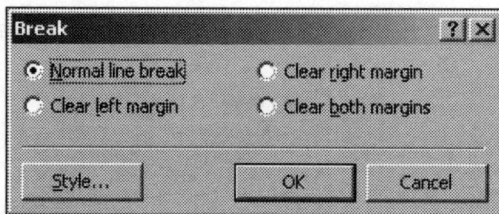

Horizontal Line

This inserts a horizontal line at the cursor position on the page, double-clicking the line displays the following dialog box which enables you to make changes to the line.

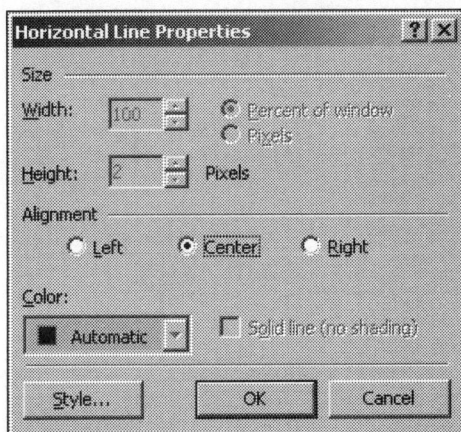

If you have applied a **theme** to the page, you can only alter the alignment of the line.

Inline Frame

Creates a frame within the current page (at the cursor position).

Date and Time

This inserts the date/time onto a page, it is sometimes useful to show the date the page was last altered.

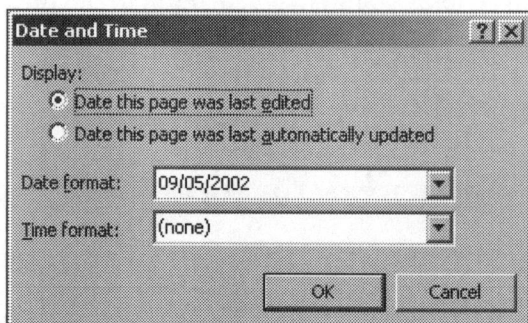

Symbol

You can insert a symbol into your page. The dialog box will remain on screen until you **Close** it.

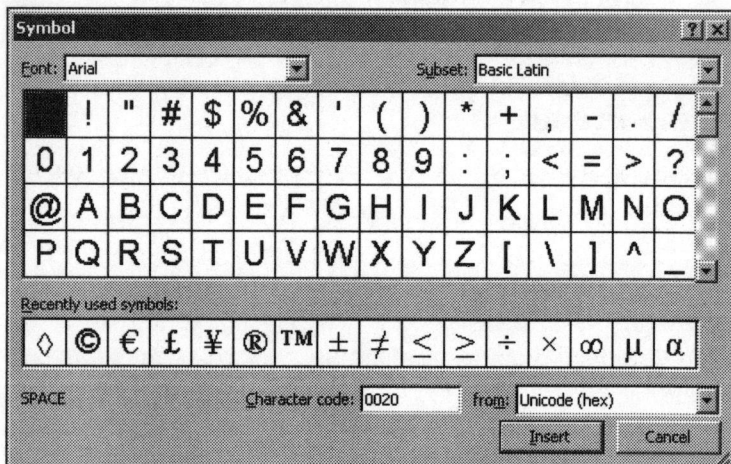

Comment

Text that will appear within FrontPage but not on the web page, it is coloured purple.

Navigation

This has been extended to include a variety of navigation and other **Web Components** that can be added to the page.

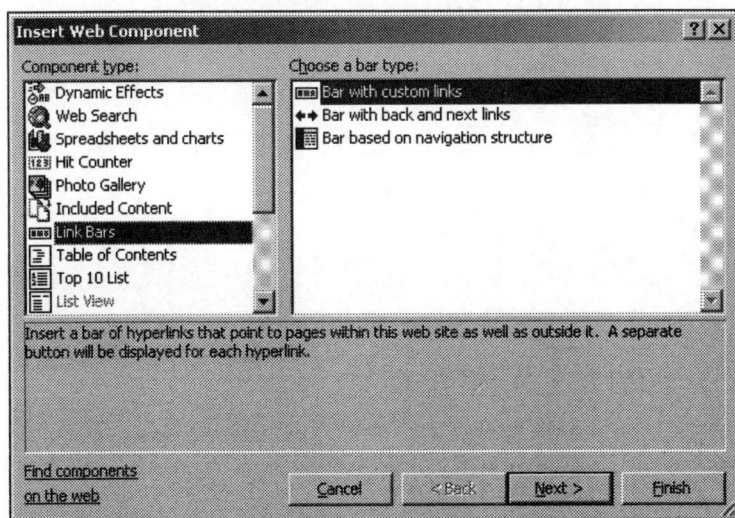

To add navigation buttons, select the **Bars based on navigation structure**, make the layout choices and click the **Finish** button.

From the display choose the navigation you want (this can be altered at any time by highlighting the navigation bar and going through the process again).

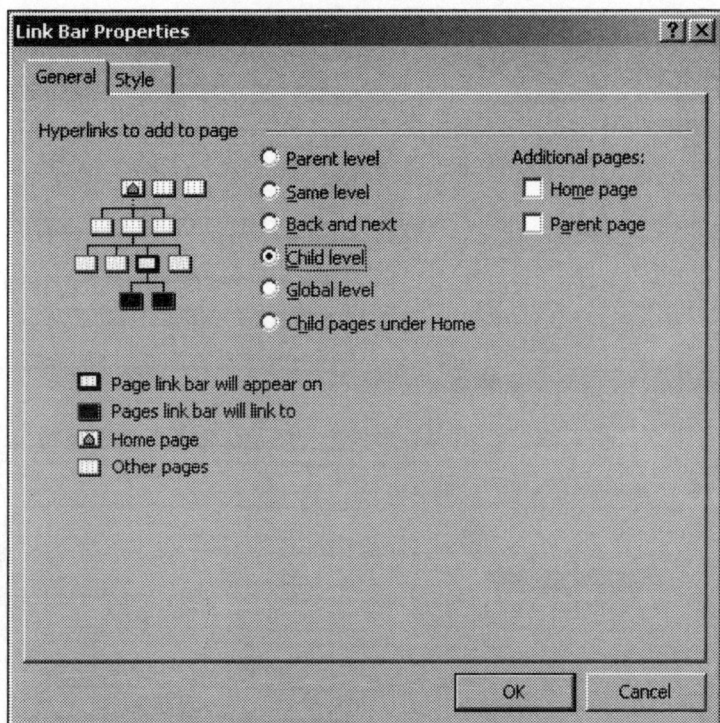

You can include a navigation bar to other pages on your web or to external (e.g. child) webs.

The bar will appear at the current cursor position (if you want the navigation bar to appear on every page then you must include it in the upper or lower third of the page (above or below the **Shared Borders**).

Make sure when choosing the options (e.g. **Parent Page**) that you are able to move around your web in the way you intend.

If you want to alter the choices, highlight the **Navigation Bar** you have inserted and go through the process again.

Page Banner

This inserts a page banner (usually in the top **Shared Border**) in the page.

In a similar way to **Navigation Bars** the banner will appear on every page containing the border.

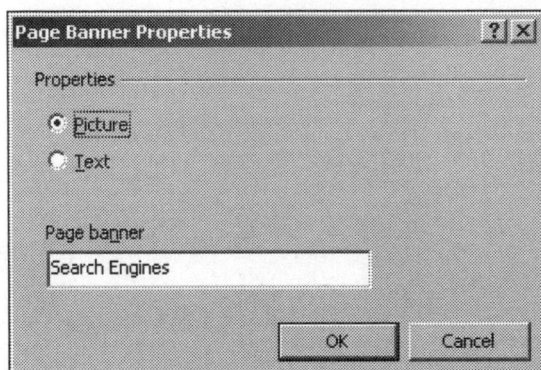

Component

This enables you to insert any of the listed components into your current page.

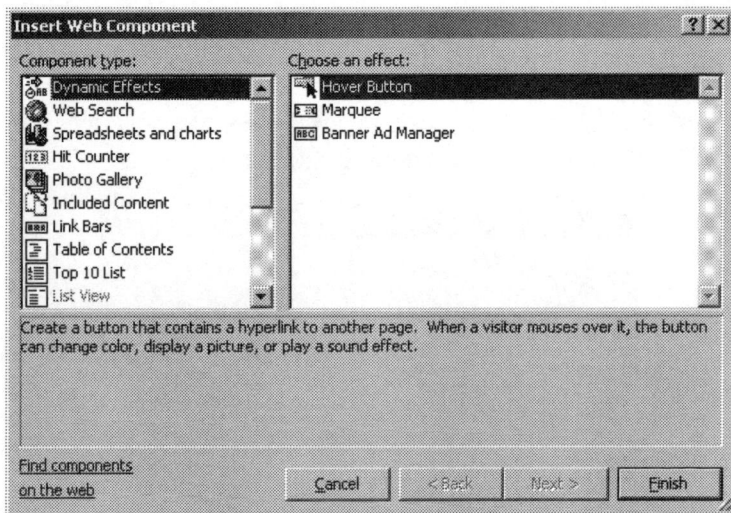

Insert Web Component dialog box:

Component type:
- Dynamic Effects
- Web Search
- Spreadsheets and charts
- Hit Counter
- Photo Gallery
- Included Content
- Link Bars
- Table of Contents
- Top 10 List
- List View

Choose an effect:
- Hover Button
- Marquee
- Banner Ad Manager

Create a button that contains a hyperlink to another page. When a visitor mouses over it, the button can change color, display a picture, or play a sound effect.

Find components on the web

Cancel | < Back | Next > | Finish

Hover Button

A hover button is an animated button that is activated (colour changes, effect, etc.) when the mouse is moved over the button.

You can use this to create interesting button links to other pages.

Marquee

This is the name given to the creation of scrolling text on a (coloured) background. You enter the text you want to use and alter the settings as desired.

Please do not over-use this feature, it may look good initially but can become tedious in time.

To alter an existing **Marquee**, double-click it.

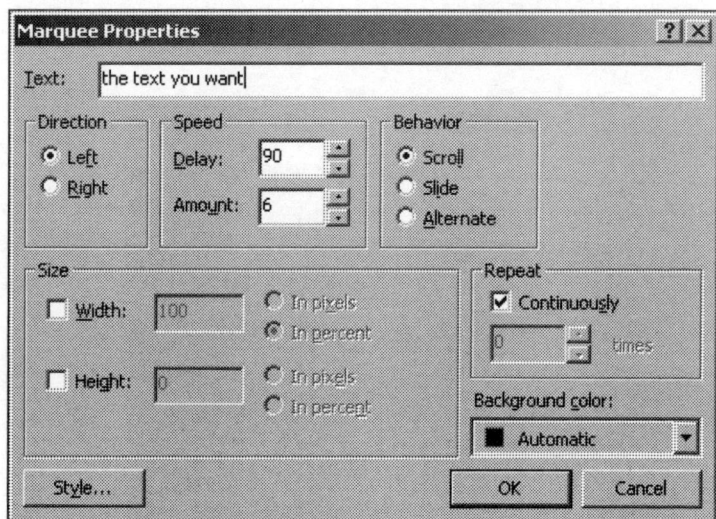

Banner Ad Manager

You will have seen banner advertisements on many commercial web pages, they display for several seconds and then another advertisement is shown and then the display reverts back to the original and so on.

You can organise banner advertisements using this command.

Be careful to use images that are of a similar size and make sure that you have chosen width and height settings that show all of the advertisement.

Hit Counter

A hit counter records how many people have accessed your site; it only appears (properly) when you have uploaded your pages to the Internet or Intranet server.

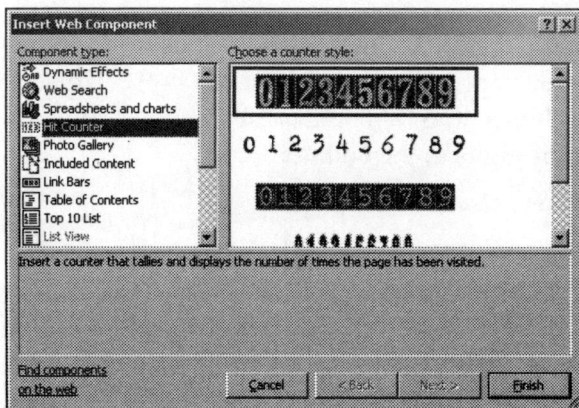

You can select one of the counters shown or you can use your own GIF image.

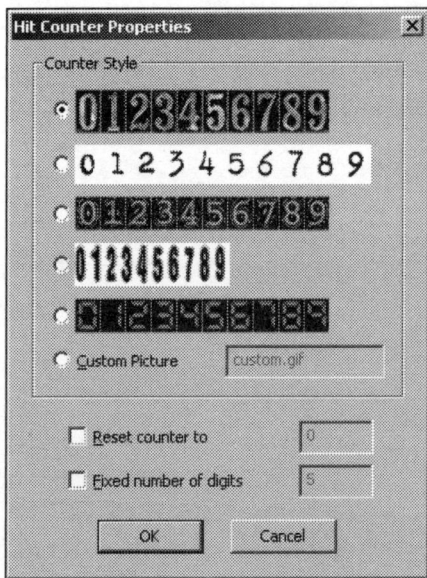

You can set the counter starting position. It has been known for sites to set the counter to (say) 5976 so that the viewer thinks it is a popular site. You can also set the number of digits in the counter.

Photo Gallery

A quick and effective way of including several pictures within the page.

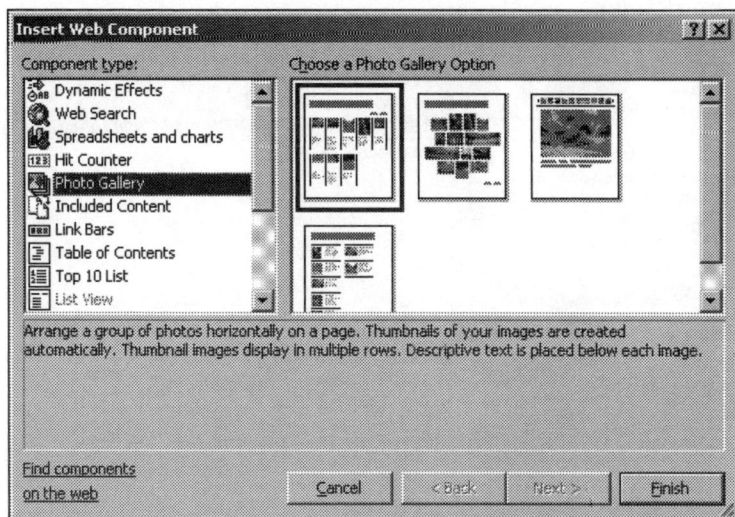

Table of contents

An automatic table of contents can be included on any page (although it makes sense to position it on the index (first) page.

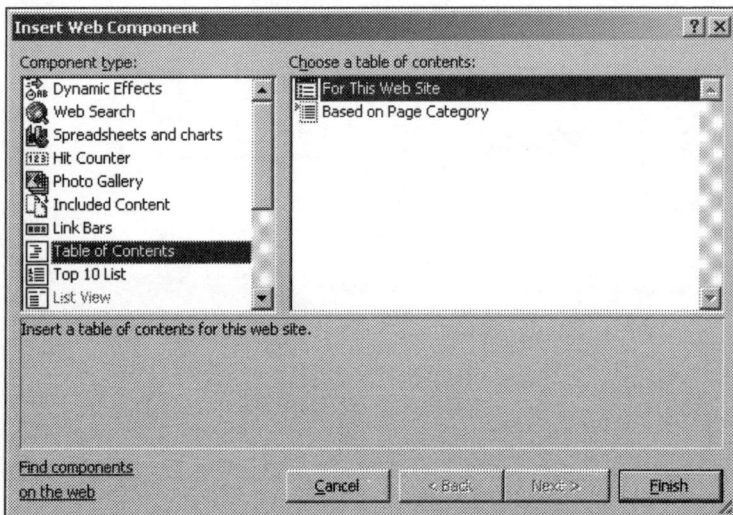

The table will be shown as headings within FrontPage.

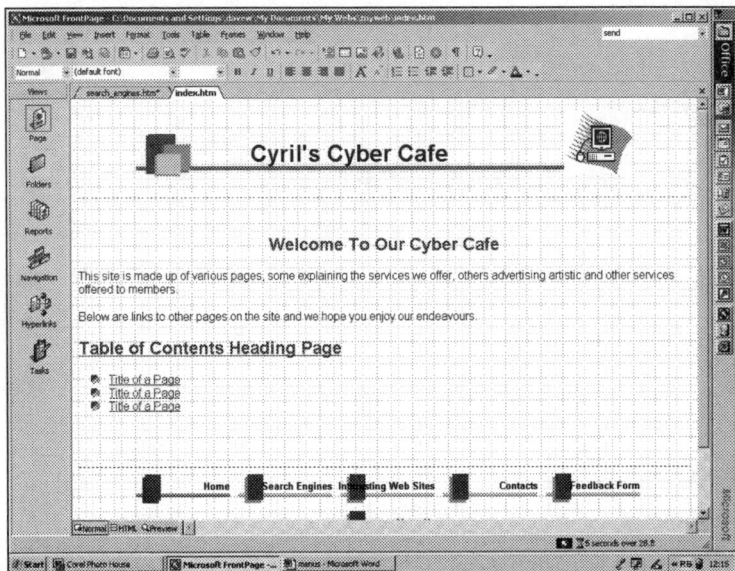

When viewed in the browser, the table of contents will be displayed.

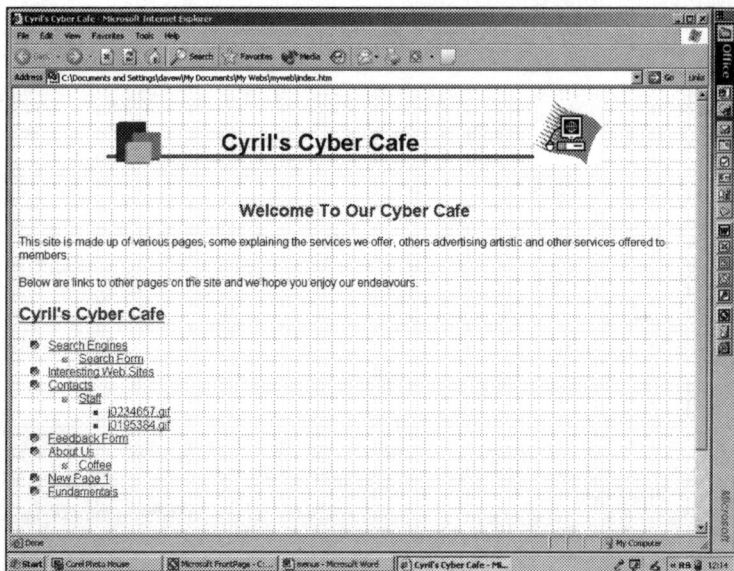

Search Form

You can set up a search tool to let the user search for text within your web site.

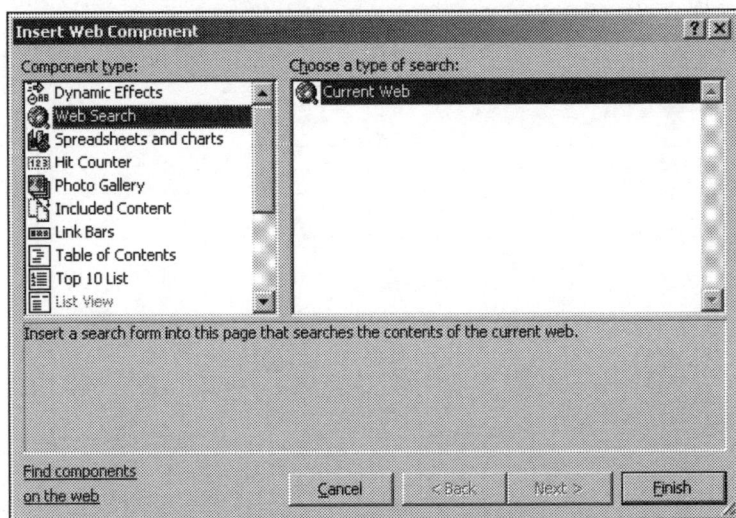

You can alter the look of the search and also alter the way in which the results are displayed by selecting the **Search Results** tab in the dialog box.

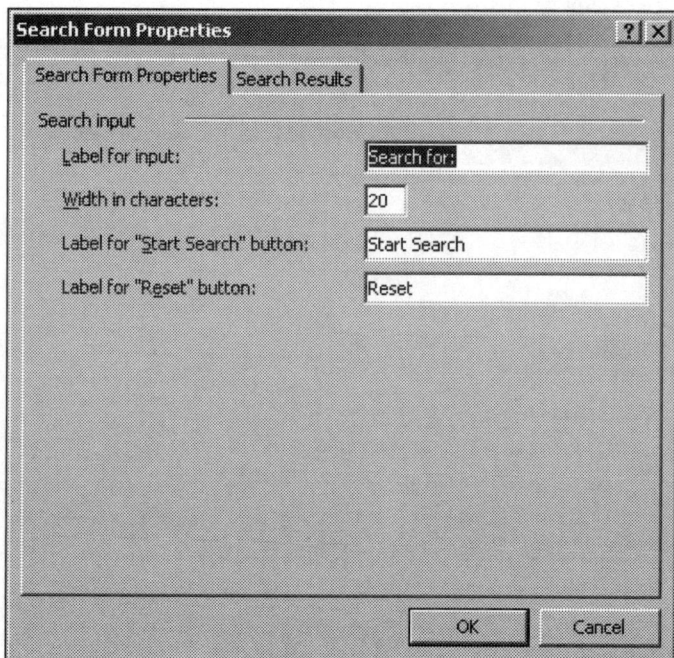

Search Form Properties	? X

Search Form Properties | Search Results

Search input

Label for input: Search for:

Width in characters: 20

Label for "Start Search" button: Start Search

Label for "Reset" button: Reset

OK   Cancel

An example of how this appears in the browser is shown
below.

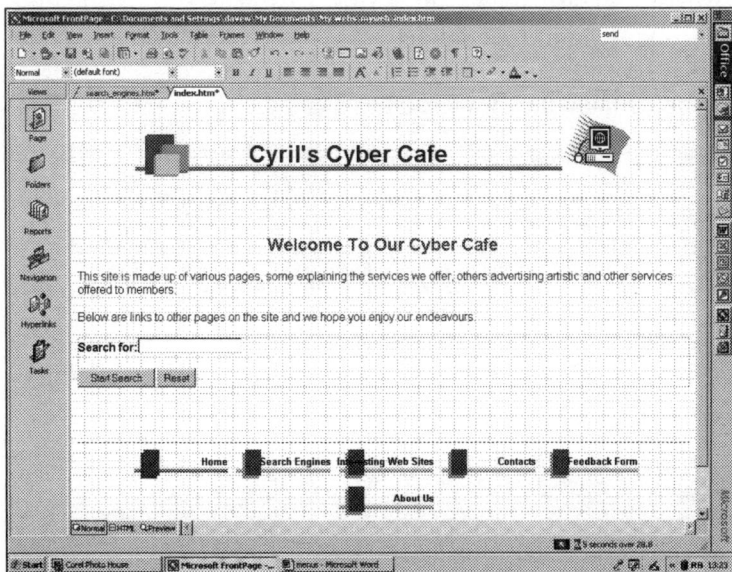

This feature requires a web server supporting **FrontPage
Extensions**.

Database

Use the wizard to set up a link (using SQL – structured query language) to a database.

The web page has to be renamed.

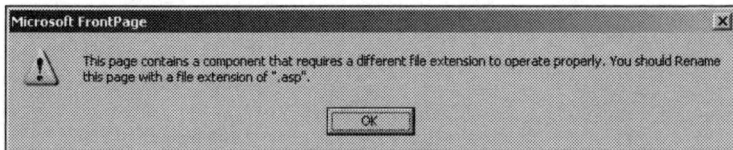

The finished result is shown below; however the web must be hosted on a server that supports **Active Server Pages** for the page to work properly.

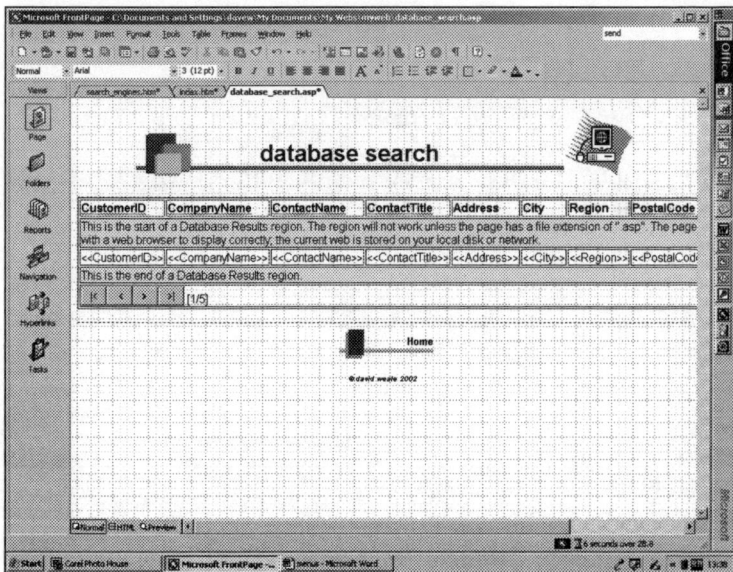

Form

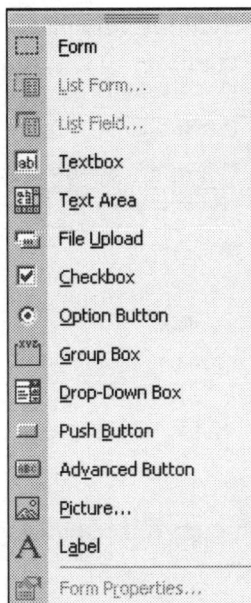

You can create forms on your pages which the user can fill in and submit replies.

This would be useful for any information-collecting exercises, e.g. customer satisfaction surveys, requests for information and so on.

Picture

An image can be inserted into the page.

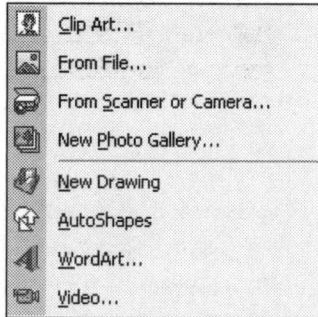

Pictures from any of these sources can be inserted into the current page.

Please remember that copyright laws apply to any images.

From File

This enables you to look for other files on your hard discs, on the Internet or Intranet.

The Internet contains many sites that contain free images including animated gifs to enliven your site.

There is a toolbar button to insert a picture from file.

File

This inserts an HTML file into the current page; you can also insert various other types of file (which are automatically converted into HTML) or drag and drop from Windows Explorer into FrontPage.

Bookmark

You can set bookmarks on a page, which enable you to quickly go to a specific part of the page (or to a bookmark on another page – provided there is a hyperlink to the bookmark on that page).

To create a bookmark, pull down the **Insert** menu, click **Bookmark**. In the **Bookmark name** box, type the name of the bookmark.

To go to a bookmark, in **Page** view, click **Bookmark** on the **Insert** menu. In the **Other bookmarks on this page** box, click the bookmark you want to find. Click **Goto**.

Hyperlink

Inserts a hyperlink at the cursor position; you can
enter both the text that will appear on the page
and the actual link within the dialog box.

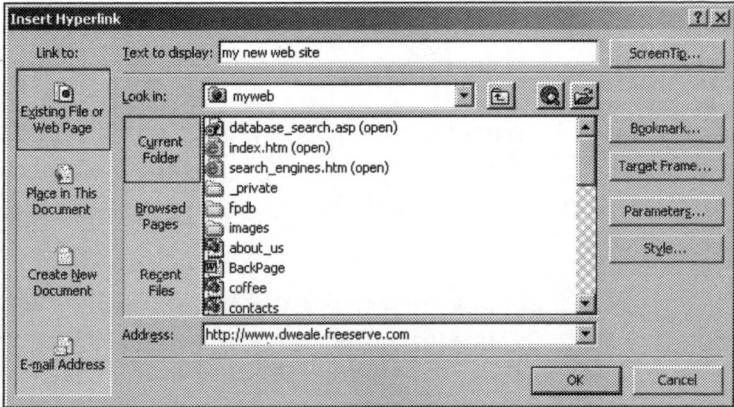

Alternatively, type the text for the hyperlink (on the page)
and then highlight the text before creating the link using
the toolbar button.

Remember that hyperlink text needs to be meaningful.

This creates a text link, however you may like to consider
using either **Hover Buttons** or **Navigation Bars** as a more
professional and visual alternative.

Images as hyperlinks

You can create a hyperlink from an image, e.g. a button or picture, by clicking on the image and then clicking on the (toolbar) hyperlink button.

Any image you use should include some explanatory text or it should be obvious where the link is pointing.

Hotspots

You do not need to include the entire image as a single hyperlink; you can use part of it as a link by defining that part as a hotspot using the hotspot buttons on the **Picture** toolbar to define the section of the image.

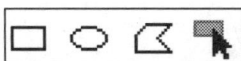

The first three buttons are to define the hotspot area within the selected graphic; the fourth highlights the existing hotspot.

If you want to be adventurous, you could define several hotspots on a single image, for example you could create individual hotspots for each county within a map of England with the links going to a page devoted to each county.

Format

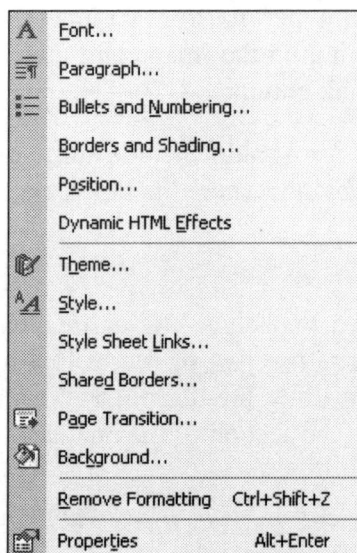

A	Font...	
	Paragraph...	
	Bullets and Numbering...	
	Borders and Shading...	
	Position...	
	Dynamic HTML Effects	
	Theme...	
	Style...	
	Style Sheet Links...	
	Shared Borders...	
	Page Transition...	
	Background...	
	Remove Formatting	Ctrl+Shift+Z
	Properties	Alt+Enter

Font

You can alter the font properties of selected text using this command.

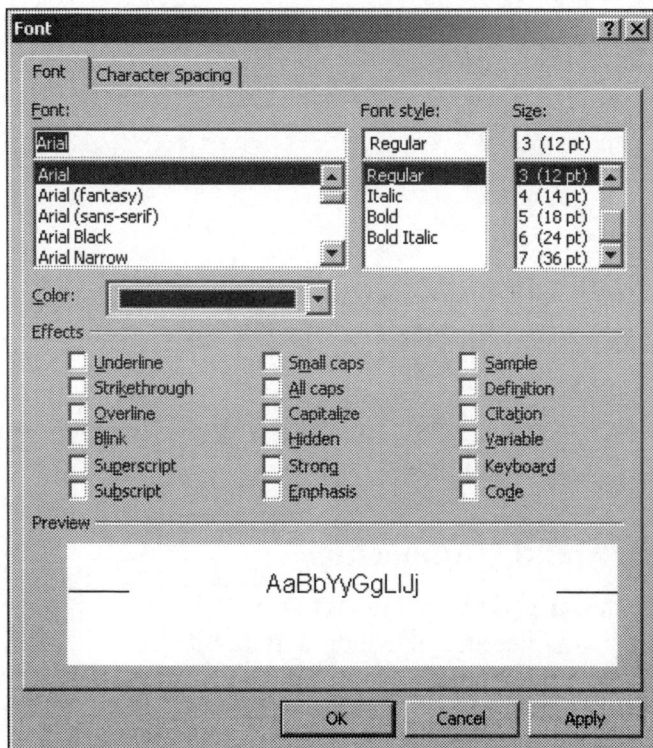

You can alter the **Character Spacing**, which can be useful at times.

There are buttons on the toolbar, which do some of the same formatting.

| Normal | ▾ | Arial | ▾ | 3 (12 pt) | ▾ | **B** | *I* | U̲ |

Paragraph

You can alter the paragraph formatting by altering alignment, spacing, indents and so on.

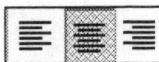

You can also use this command with other items on the page, e.g. hover buttons.

Bullets and Numbering

There are a variety of numbered or bulleted styles available, any of which can be altered using the **Style** button.

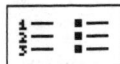

Borders and Shading

You can add borders and shading to your pages in a very similar way to a word processing program.

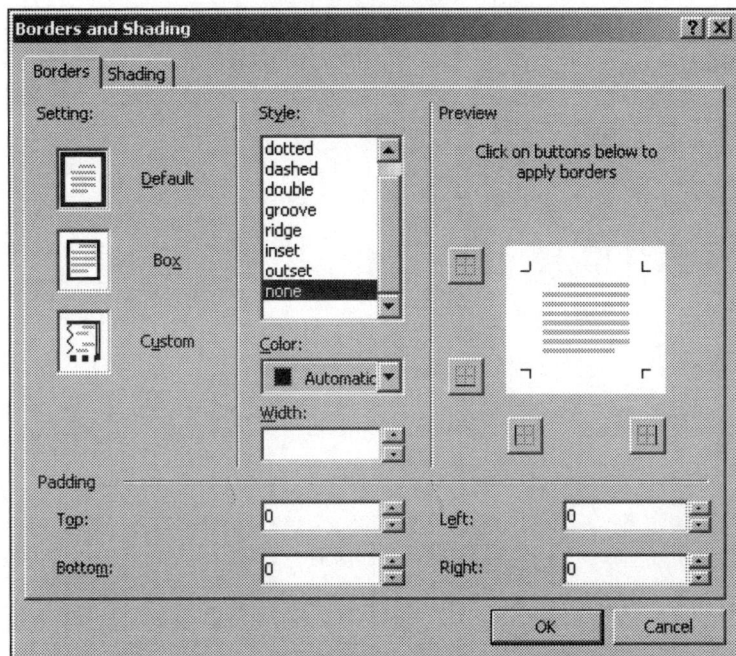

Position

This command lets you decide upon the alignment of images (relative to the text on the page).

This can be useful, however it is often better to use **Tables** for layout as they allow a more sophisticated result.

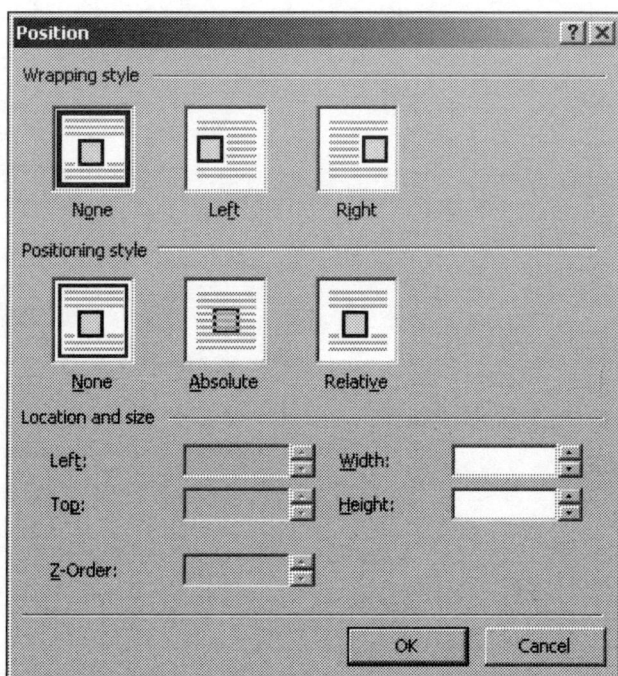

Dynamic HTML Effects

You can select different animations for text and images.

For example you can animate a picture so that when the mouse moves over that picture another picture appears or you can make selected text swirl onto the page when the page loads.

To do this, select the image or text, pull down the **Format** menu and select **Dynamic HTML Effects (DHTML)**.

Pull down each of the choices and select the one you want to use (the choices depend upon whether you have selected text or an image).

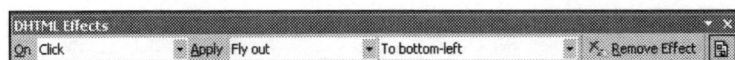

DHTML Effects				▼ ×
On: Click	Apply: Fly out	To bottom-left	Remove Effect	

The effects will become apparent when you view the page in the browser.

Theme

You can apply a theme to a page or an entire web; the theme sets the appearance of the pages and can be modified.

It is possible to add (or remove) a theme from **All Pages** or from **Selected Pages**.

To remove a theme select the (**No Theme**) option from the list again, either selecting **All Pages** or **Selected Pages**.

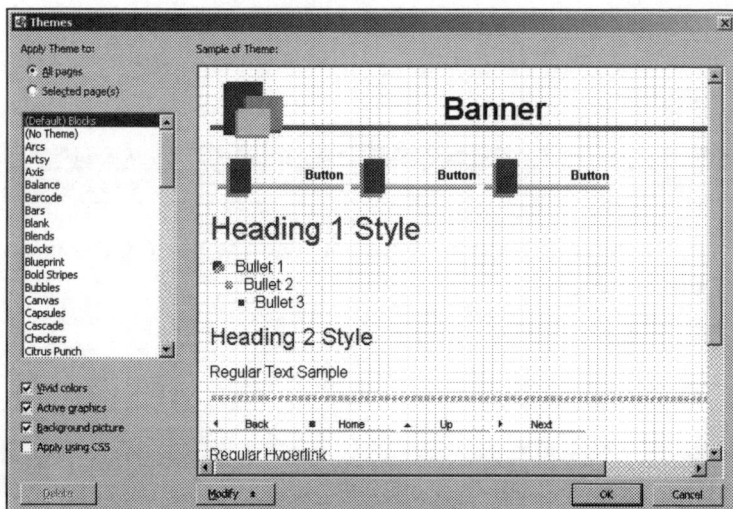

The **Modify** button enables various options to allow you to customise the appearance of the theme.

Themes are a way of making your web look professional in a relatively painless way.

Modifying themes

Once you click the **Modify** button, you will be given the choice of altering the **Colors**, **Graphics** or **Text**.

For example if you want to alter the look or font for the navigation buttons, then select **Graphics** and you can alter the image or font for the buttons.

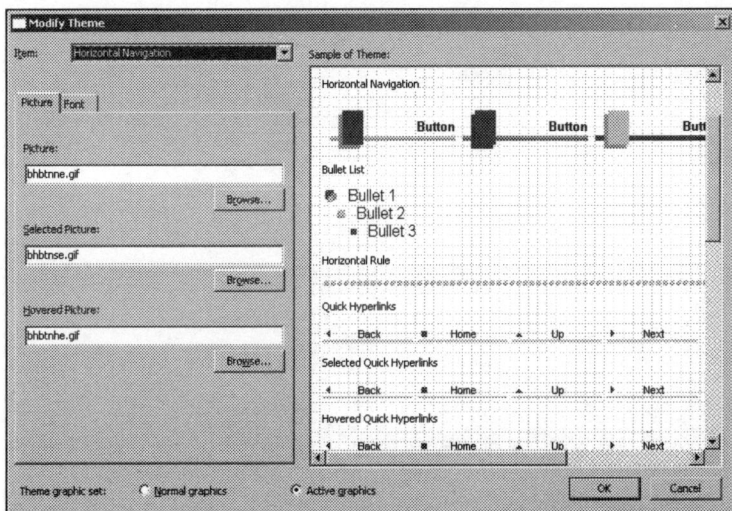

The theme will be saved as a copy of the original (this avoids writing over the original theme). Using the **Save As** option lets you choose a new name for the modified theme.

143

Style

You can change the default style of any of the listed **html** tags. You can create a new style or modify a style.

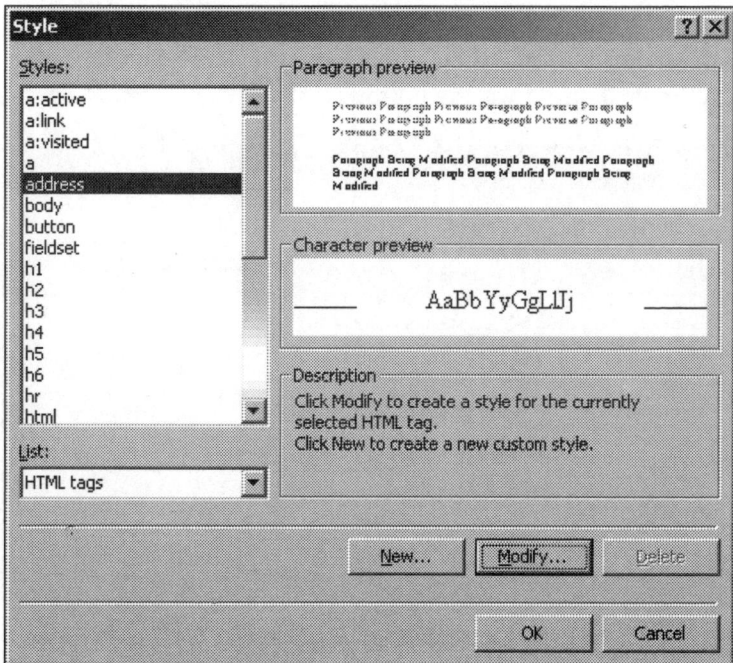

Stylesheet Links

A stylesheet is a method of precisely setting the formatting of a web site. The formatting instructions are held in the stylesheet and then can be imposed on a page or series of pages. This command links the page to a stylesheet. Not all browsers support stylesheets.

Shared Borders

This creates shared borders for pages on the web site.

The default is shown below, you can add or take away borders as you choose by clicking to insert or remove a tick in the boxes.

You can add or take away these borders on individual pages by using the **Current page** option.

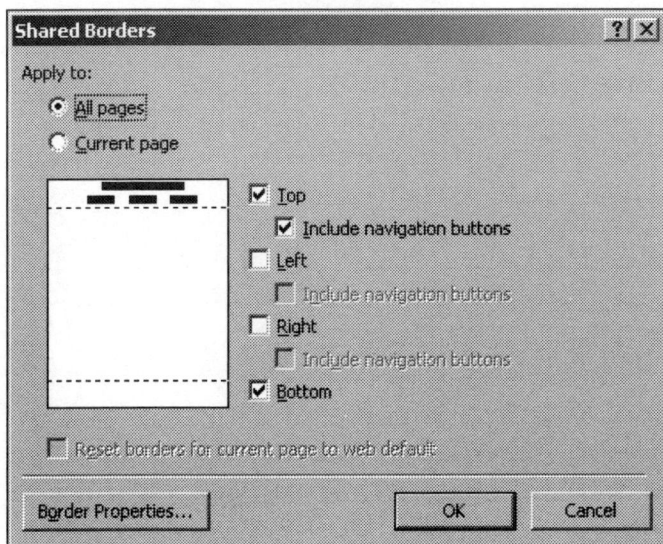

Page Transition

A transition is the special effect used when a page is loaded or the user moves onto another page.

You can make various adjustments to the settings shown in the dialog box.

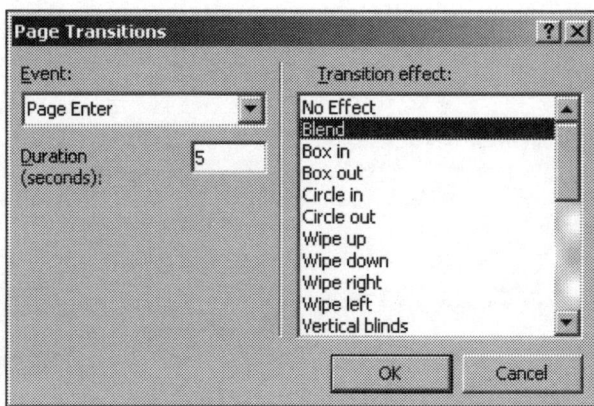

Background

This is only available if there is no theme applied to the web.

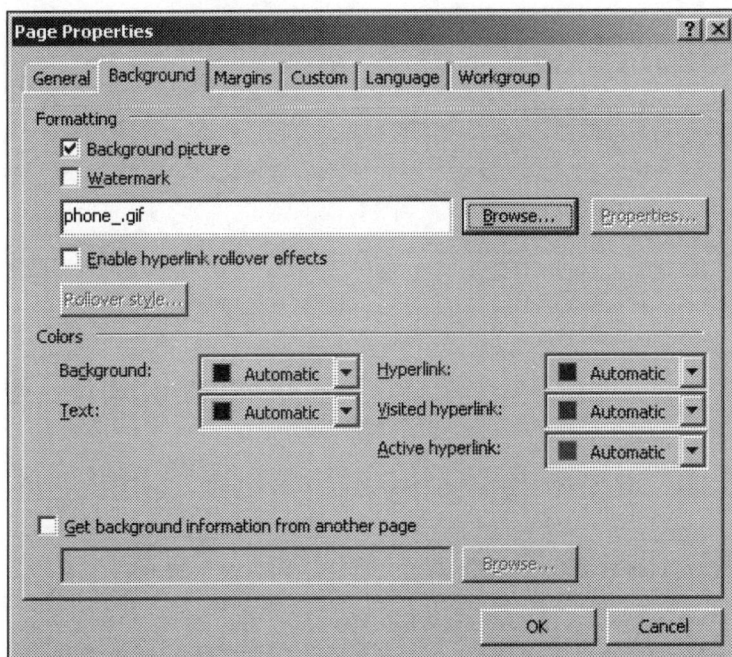

If you decide to add a background image then please make sure that the user can still read the text easily.

As can be seen from the next illustration, images can easily obscure the text.

Remove Formatting

This removes the formatting from selected text.

Properties

You can alter the properties of the selected item. The dialog box differs (as do the properties) depending upon whether you have selected text or an image, etc.

Tools

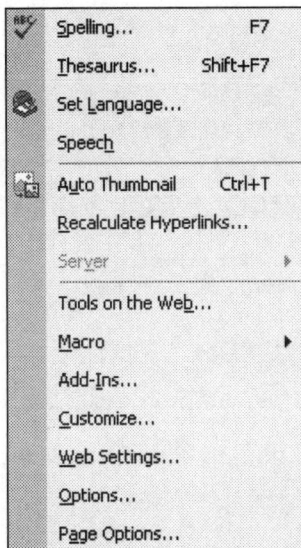

	Spelling...	F7
Thesaurus...	Shift+F7
Set Language...	
Speech	
Auto Thumbnail	Ctrl+T
Recalculate Hyperlinks...	
Server	▶
Tools on the Web...	
Macro	▶
Add-Ins...	
Customize...	
Web Settings...	
Options...	
Page Options...	

Spelling

This checks your spelling and is a vital tool. There is nothing more likely to detract from the professionalism of your site than poorly spelt contents.

In **Navigator** view you can choose to spell-check all or selected pages. (In **Page** view the normal spellchecker is loaded and just checks that page).

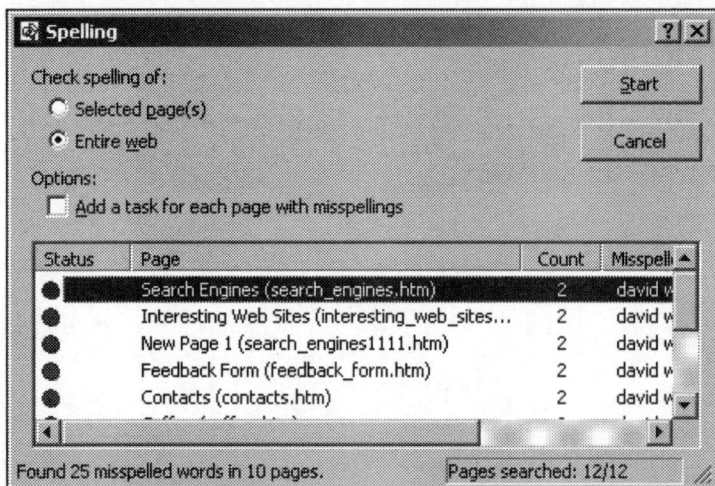

You can tick the box to Add a task for each page with misspellings.

This does not correct the spelling mistakes as you go through the file but merely identifies them for later alteration.

When you carry out the **task**, the normal spell checking automatically kicks in.

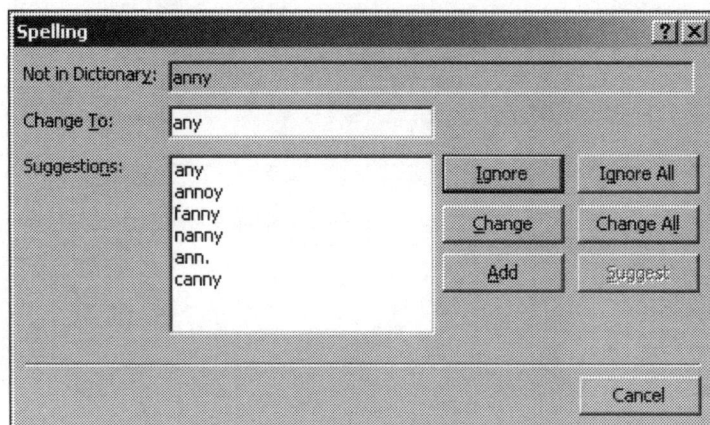

Spelling	? X

Not in Dictionary: anny

Change To: any

Suggestions:
any
annoy
fanny
nanny
ann.
canny

Ignore   Ignore All

Change   Change All

Add   Suggest

Cancel

You can **Add** words not in the current dictionary; this is useful for names and technical words specific to your site.

The **F7** function key also activates the spellchecker.

Thesaurus

If you want to find another word with a similar meaning, this is a useful tool.

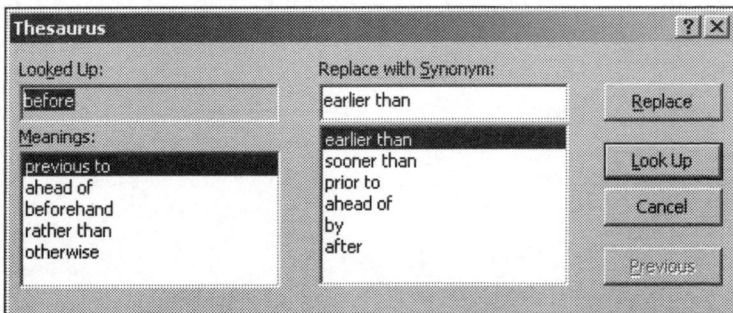

You need to select the word you want to find an alternative to and you can also use **Shift** and **F7** (hold the first key while pressing the second) to load the thesaurus.

Set Language

It is possible to set a different language for *highlighted* text using this command.

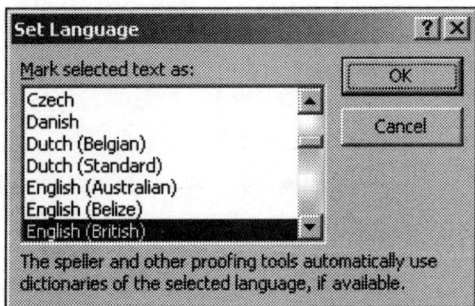

Speech

Office XP has speech recognition facilities (using a microphone as input, the program has to be trained to recognise the voice).

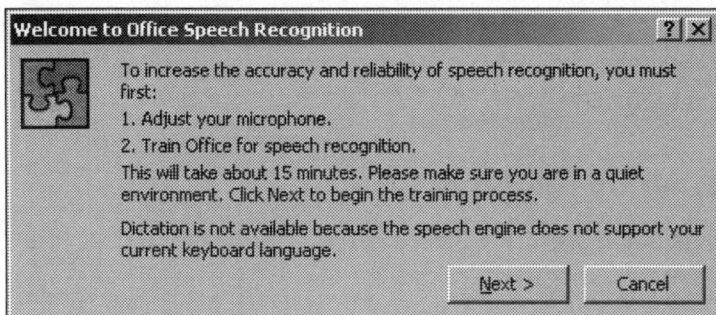

Auto Thumbnail

A thumbnail is a miniature version of the image; clicking on the thumbnail loads the original picture (you will need to use the **Back** button on the browser toolbar to return to the original page).

To create a thumbnail, select the image. Use the menu option or click the **Auto Thumbnail** button on the **Pictures** toolbar.

You will not be able to create a thumbnail if the original picture is smaller than the thumbnail settings (or if it is a hyperlink).

To adjust the thumbnail setting, use the **Page Options** settings in the **Tools** menu.

Recalculate Hyperlinks

This recalculates internal links (this means links to pages within the site as opposed to links to external pages or sites) when they have become broken (where the link no longer exists).

Tools on the Web

This connects to the Microsoft web site and enables you to access various tools.

Macro

You can create macros just like within other applications.

Add-Ins

Add-ins are supplemental programs to add commands and features. You can download some add-ins from the Microsoft web site or from independent software suppliers, e.g. shareware.

Customize

Standard options to add/remove buttons, etc., and to make the toolbars reflect the way you work.

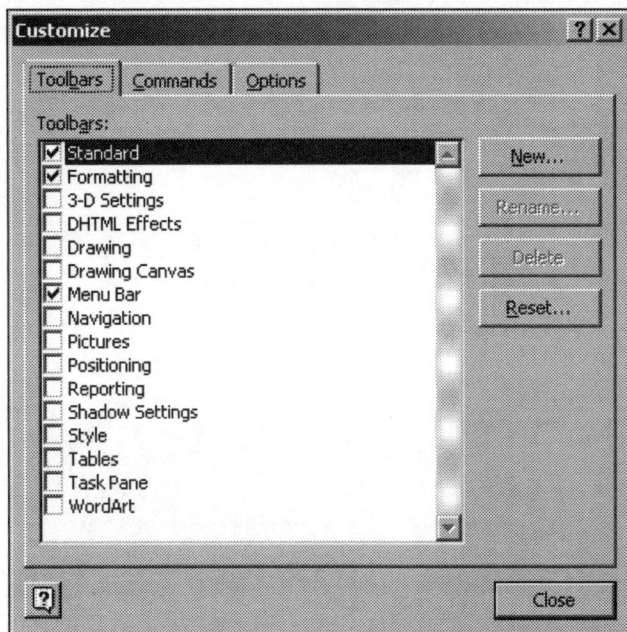

To add buttons to the toolbars, use the commands tab, select the **Category** followed by the **Command** and drag the button to any available toolbar.

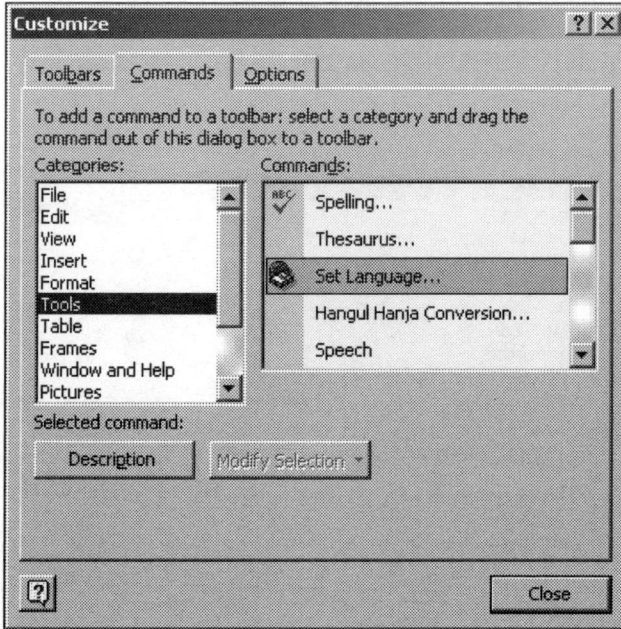

To remove a button, drag it away from the toolbar (this will only work when the dialog box (above) is displayed.

Web Settings

You can alter various default settings for your web, e.g. the text on the navigation buttons (**Navigation** tab).

Options

Here changes can be made to some of the configuration
settings, e.g. to the defaults for publishing the web.

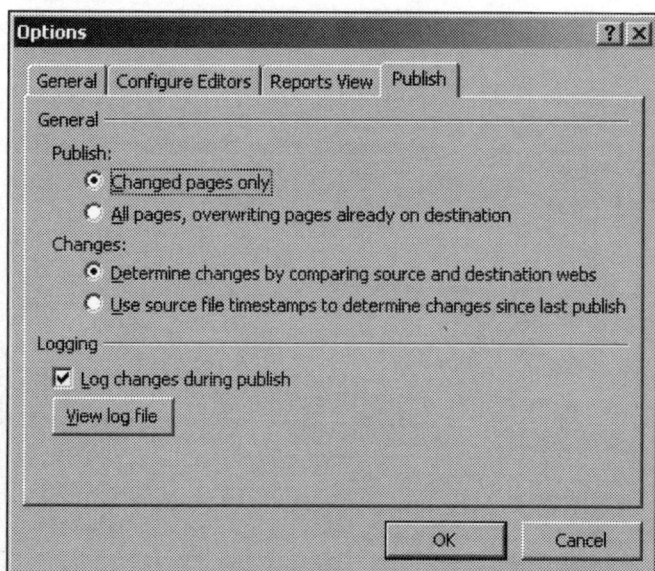

Page Options

Here you can make changes to the default settings for pages, e.g. alter the **AutoThumbnail** settings.

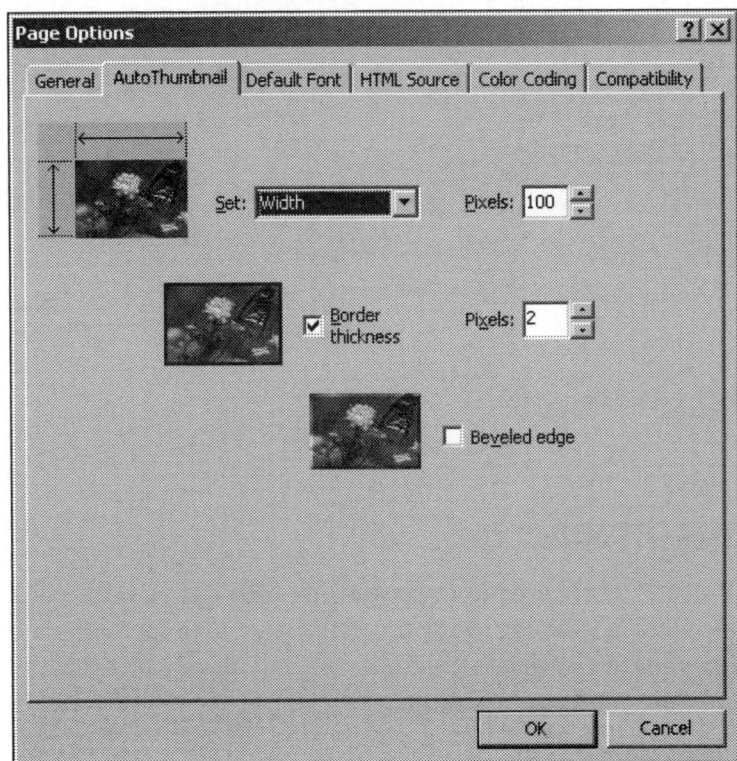

Table menu

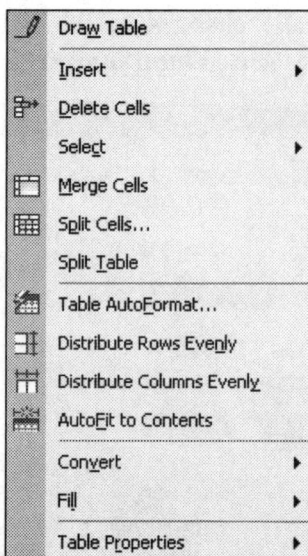

Draw Table

You can draw a table (freehand) by clicking and dragging the cursor, starting with the table and then drawing the lines for the rows and columns, the only problem is that the columns may not be symmetric.

Here is an example I drew.

Insert

You can insert four different items.

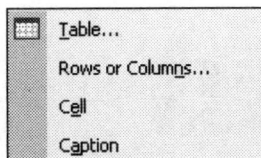

Table

This lets you specify the layout of the table.

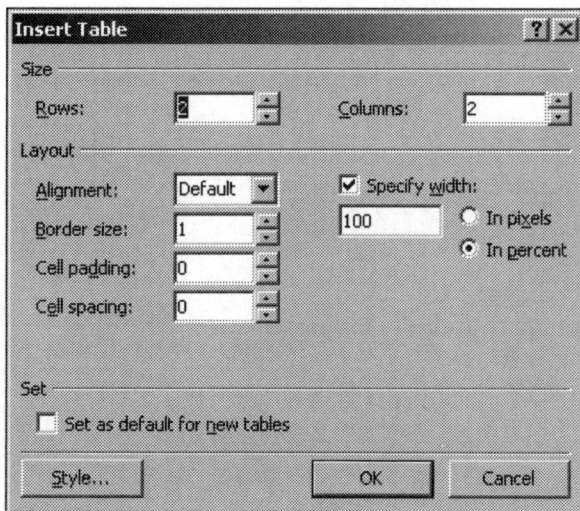

The table will appear at the current cursor position.

As an alternative, the toolbar button makes use of a grid to create the table.

Cell Padding refers to space (in pixels) between the contents and the sides of the cells; this cannot be set for individual cells but applies to the whole table.

Cell Spacing is the spacing (in pixels) between the individual cells in the table.

You can, if you wish, insert a table within the cell of an existing table to create special effects.

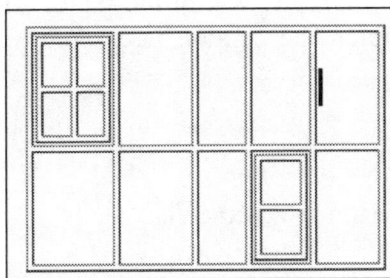

Row or Columns

You can insert rows or columns into your table at the cursor position.

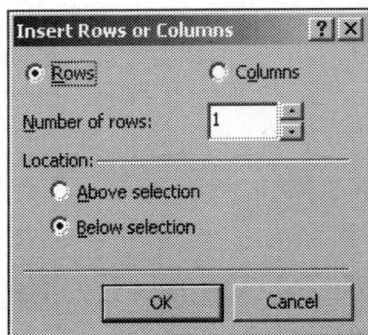

Cell

This inserts an additional cell to the right of the current cell.

Caption

As long as the cursor is within the table, you can insert a title for the table. The caption is centred above the table (by default).

Delete Cells

This will delete the **selected** cells.

Select

You can select the whole table, a column (or columns), a row (or rows) and a cell (or cells).

Merge Cells

The **selected** cells will be merged into one cell.

Split Cells

This splits a cell into two.

Distribute Rows/Columns Evenly

Spaces the selected rows or columns symmetrically.

AutoFit to Contents

Automatically fits the cells to the contents.

Convert

Text To Table

This converts the selected text into a table; how the text is separated into cells is defined within the dialog box.

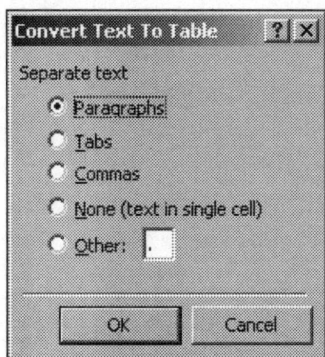

Convert Table To Text

Converts the contents of a table into text, each cell becoming a separate line.

Properties

You can alter various properties of the table, cell or caption.

Table

Similar to **Cell Properties** but applies to the whole table.

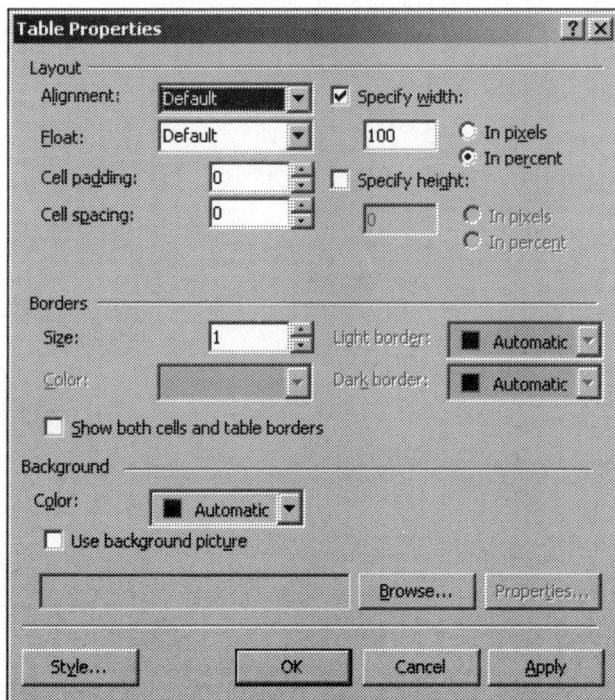

The **Size** (if defined in percentage terms) means that the table will resize to fit within the browser's window, if defined in pixels it may not fit.

Cell

You use this to define the layout and style of the **selected** cells.

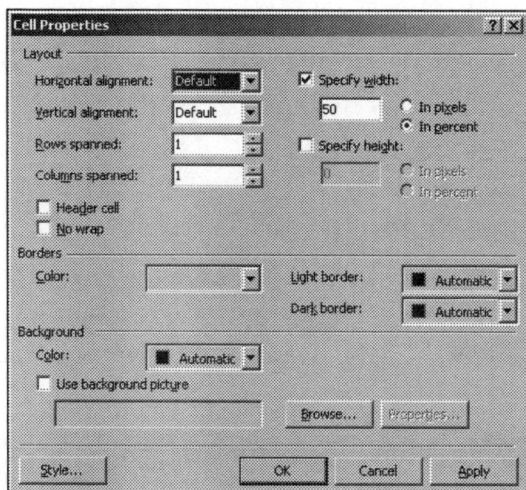

Header Cell, if this is selected then the text within the cell will be in bold.

No Wrap, if you select this, the text will not wrap around within the cell (when viewed within a browser).

If you choose to include a **background picture** then make sure the contents of the cell are still easily read.

Caption

This enables you to position the table caption and to alter the **Style** (using the button).

Frames

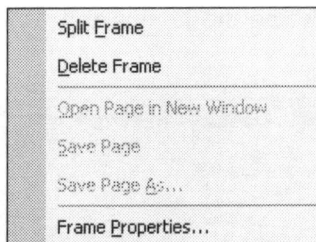

| Split Frame |
| Delete Frame |
| Open Page in New Window |
| Save Page |
| Save Page As... |
| Frame Properties... |

Creating a frame page

Before this menu can be used, a frame page has to be created (**File**, **New**, **Page or Web**, **Page Templates**, **Frames Pages**), finally selecting the type of frame page desired.

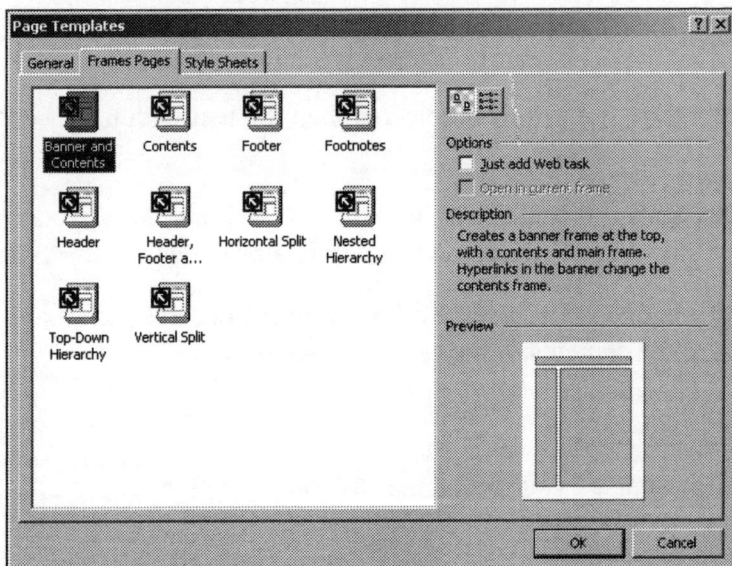

An example of a frame page is shown below.

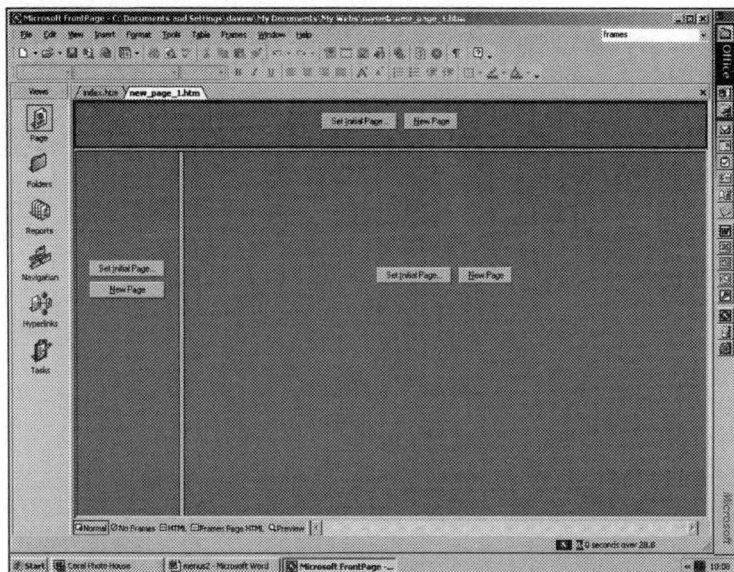

Use the **Set Initial Page** button to determine the page which will appear in this frame, the **New Page** button enables you to create a page if it does not already exist.

Split Frame

This enables you to split the current frame into two, creating a new frame.

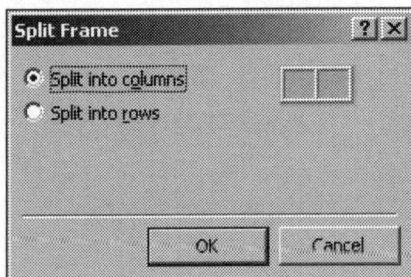

Delete Frame

Deletes the current frame.

Open Page in New Window

This opens the current page in a new window. You can use the **Back** and **Forwards** buttons to return to the previous screen.

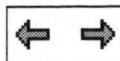

Save Page / Save Page As

Saves the current page (**Save As** gives you the option of saving it to another location or under a different name).

Frame Properties

You can set certain properties and styles for the frame.

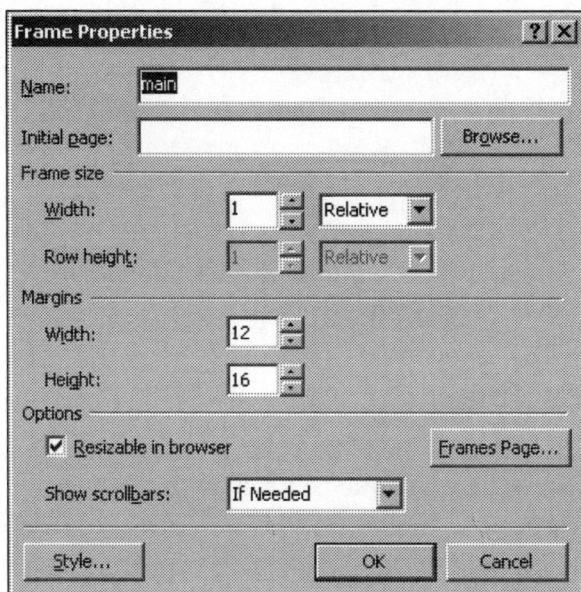

Window

New Window

Creates a new window.

Help

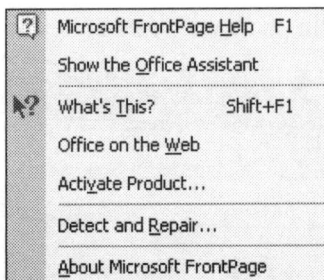

The help screens are similar to those found in other Windows programs.

What's This

Click on this and then drag the question mark over the area or item you want help with.

Office on the Web

Loads your browser and links to the Microsoft site.

Detect and Repair

This checks and repairs the program installation (you may need the CD for this).

Other Toolbar Buttons

There are some buttons not available in the pull-down menus.

Format Painter

You use this to copy formatting from one part of the page to another.

Highlight or select the item, click the button and then drag the mouse over the text or object to be formatted.

Show All

This displays all the hidden (non-printing) characters and is useful to explain why the page doesn't look quite the way you thought it should.

Stop

This button stops the activity (e.g. the loading of web pages); it can be used when you get bored waiting for a page to load.

HTML Tutorial

This is an introduction to HTML coding, so that you can alter the code generated by FrontPage.

It is intended as an overview. If you want to extend your knowledge of HTML, for example frames or forms, there are many books or Internet sites that can assist you.

Fundamentals of HTML files

All HTML files follow a fixed structure.

```
<html>
<head>
<title>an example of the use of html</title>
</head>
<body>
the contents of your page
</body>
</html>
```

As you can see the structure is created by the use of **tags**, each tag begins a section of the file and there is a further tag (with a / symbol) to end that part of the structure.

The structure

<html></html>

The file begins and ends with these tags, which define it as an HTML file.

<head></head>

These tags contain the title and other information.

<title></title>

The (descriptive) title of your page is contained between these tags. Your choice of title is important, as it must give potential readers enough information about the contents (it is shown in the title bar on browsers and can appear in search engine results).

<body></body>

In this section, you enter the code to create your page.

A simple example

An example of the *body text* is shown below, which is followed by an explanation of the code.

You will need to add the rest of the structure, e.g. the head section and the html tags at beginning and end.

```
<body>
<h1> david's first page</h1>
this makes use of <b>bold text</b>
<i>italic text</i>
<tt>typewriter style text</tt>
</body>
```

The tags can be capitalised or not as you prefer.

Basic tags

<h1>

This is a first level heading, there are six heading levels (H1 to H6), H1 being the largest. Each level of heading has different formatting as well as being a different size.

Two examples are shown below.

<h1> **</h1>**	1st level heading - large, bold (with automatic line breaks and spaces)
<h5> **</h5>**	5th level heading - small (line breaks, etc., as above)

<b></b>

Any text within these tags will be in bold.

<i></i>

Text between these tags will be in italic.

<tt> </tt>

Use these if you want typewriter style text.

<strong></strong>

Strong text (very similar to heading level 4) except that there is no line break as there is with headings.

You can combine tags.

Creating a file from scratch

1. Load Windows Notepad.

2. Type in the basic structure for your file.

3. Save the file as an **html** file in whatever folder you wish (add an **htm** extension to the file, i.e. **myfirstfile.htm**). It is best to make sure that the **Filetype** box shows **All Files**.

4. Close Notepad.

5. Load Microsoft Explorer.

6. Open the file you have just created (using the **Browse** button to locate the file).

7. Pull down the **View** menu and select **Source**.

8. This will re-open **Notepad** with the tags shown.

9. Enter the code you want in the **body** section of the file.

10. **Save** the file and switch back to Explorer.

11. Click on the **Refresh** button and you will see the results of your work within **Explorer** (as if you were viewing the page on the Internet).

When you want to make changes to the page, switch back to **Notepad** and repeat steps 9 to 11 until happy.

An alternative to step 6 is to drag the file from its folder into the browser or double-click it in Windows Explorer.

Practice

Create a new file and enter the example described previously (*a simple example*) remembering to add the rest of the html structure.

Then view it in the browser.

Exercise one

☐   Create a new file using Notepad. Type in the **basic structure** (html, head tags, etc.) and then add a suitable title and the following body text.

☐   Call the file **webone.htm**

```
<body>
<h1>this is a level 1 heading</h1>
<h2>this is a level 2 heading</h2>
<h3>this is a level 3 heading</h3>
<h4>this is a level 4 heading</h4>
<h5>this is a level 5 heading</h5>
<h6>this is a level 6 heading</h6>
</body>
```

The results should look similar to this when viewed in the browser.

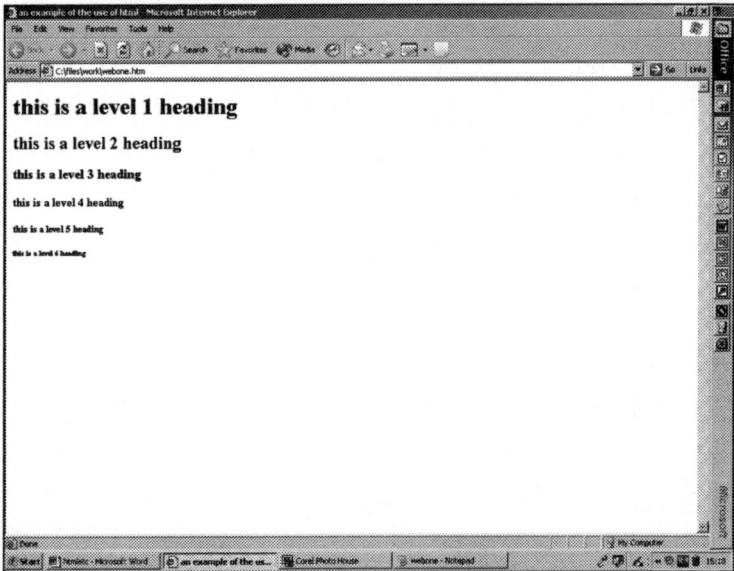

```
<html>

<head>

<title> an example of the use of html </title>

</head>

<body>

<h1>this is a level 1 heading</h1>

<h2>this is a level 2 heading</h2>

<h3>this is a level 3 heading</h3>

<h4>this is a level 4 heading</h4>

<h5>this is a level 5 heading</h5>

<h6>this is a level 6 heading</h6>

</body>

</html>
```

Formatting tags

We have already looked at some of the formatting tags (bold, italic and so on). Here are some more for you to use (**n** means a number).

Remember the text to be formatted has to be included within the tags.

<u></u>

Underlines the text.

<pre></pre>

Pre-formatted text, any text within these tags will be laid out exactly as it appears within the tags. So, if you use tabs then these will be retained.

<center></center>

Centres the text within the tags, note the spelling.

<font size=n></font>

The choice is from 1 (smallest) to 7 (largest). This is a relative size and will depend upon the screen resolution or the browser settings.

<basefont size=n>

This sets the default font size (from 1 to 7), the default, unless you alter it, is 3. The **<font size>** setting overwrites this.

<font color="nnnnnn"></font>

You can alter the colour of words or single characters, by entering the hexadecimal code for the colour you want, e.g.

<font color="98c2f4">

This is a kind of bluish colour.

To find the hexadecimal code, you can use a program such as **Paint Shop Pro**, which can be set to display hexadecimal codes within the **Colour Pallet**, alternatively there are sites on the Internet that display colour charts with the hex codes.

<font face="nameoffont"></font>

To alter the typeface of the text, insert a font name into the tag, e.g.

<font face="arial">

Example

This example is to demonstrate how you need to turn off font settings (last font tag entered is turned off first).

```
<html>

<head><title>nested tags</title></head>

<body>

<font size=6> <font face=arial> <font color=e2380>

the font will be size 6, in arial font and coloured red

</font>

closing the last font (color) means the text reverts back to the default colour

</font>

closing off the next font (face) means the text reverts back to the default font

</font>

closing the last font (size) means the font reverts back to the default font size

</body>

</html>
```

Type it into **Notepad** and save it as **ex1.htm**. When viewed in the browser, it should look similar to this.

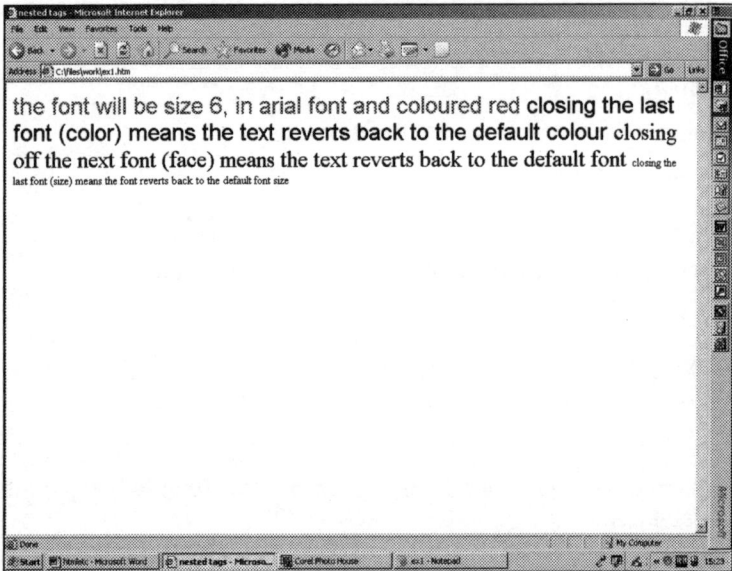

Exercise two

☐   Create a new file called **webtwo.htm** with the following body text and formatting (after creating the basic structure of the file).

I suggest you include the tag <p> to create a new paragraph between each section. This is a stand-alone tag, which exists without the need to turn it off.

```html
<html>
<head>
<title>exercise two</title>
</head>
<body>
<basefont size=5>this sets the default font size (1 to 7), the default is 3
<p>
<u>this underlines text</u>
<p>
<pre>

                preformatted text, any text within these tags will

                be laid out exactly as it appears, so you can use

                the tab key if you wish
</pre>
<p>
<font size=1>the smallest font, this command overwrites the basefont command until you close it</font>
<p>
<font size=7>the largest font size</font>
<p>
<font color=98c2f4>a blue color</font>
<p>
<font face=arial>this changes the font to arial</font>
</body>
</html>
```

This should look similar to the screen below.

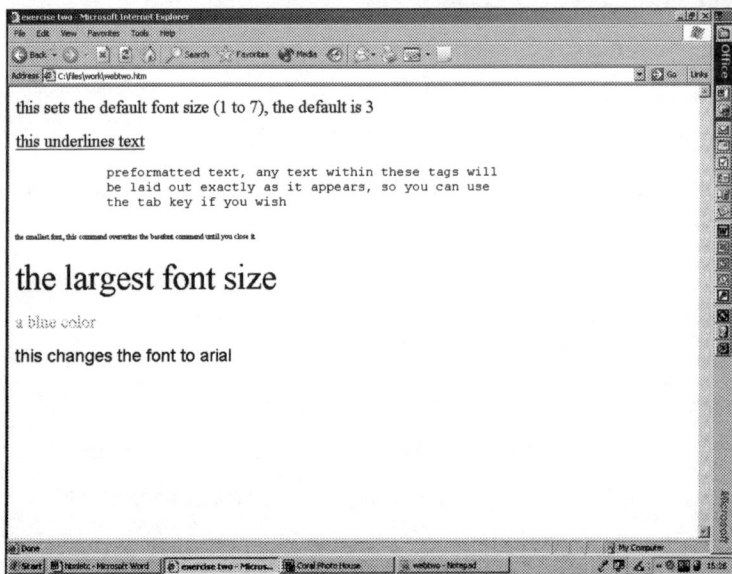

this sets the default font size (1 to 7), the default is 3

this underlines text

```
          preformatted text, any text within these tags will
          be laid out exactly as it appears, so you can use
          the tab key if you wish
```

the smallest font, this command overwrites the basefont command until you close it

the largest font size

a blue color

this changes the font to arial

Ways of creating space(s)

The following tags allow you to create space within your page.

<p></p>

The closing tag is not usually necessary. This tag creates a paragraph break with a space *before* the new paragraph. There is no point in adding more than one of these as they cannot be nested.

**
**

This begins a new line with *no* line space, however you can use multiple tags to add blank lines. There is no closing tag.

<hr>

Creates a horizontal line across the page.

<hr size=n><hr width=n> or <hr width=%>

Defines the size and width of the horizontal line in pixels (or width as a % of the page).

<hr noshade>

Produces a solid line.

<p align=center></p>

<h3 align=left></h3>

<hr align=right></hr>

These commands align paragraphs **<p align= >**, or headings **<h1 align= >**, or horizontal rules (lines) **<hr align= >** and so on.

These tags can be combined if you wish.

Exercise three

☐ Open your original file (**webone.htm**) and add the following code (shown in bold) to experiment with space and the use of horizontal lines to divide the page.

☐ When you have saved the file as **webthree.htm**, you will need to open the file in the browser.

Notice the different effects of using <p> and <br>.

```
<body>
<h1>this is a level 1 heading</h1>
<p>
<h2 align=right>this is a level 2 heading</h2>
<h3>this is a level 3 heading</h3>
<hr noshade size=50 width=50%>
<h4>this is a level 4 heading</h4><br>
<hr size=20 width=100%>
<h5>this is a level 5 heading</h5>
<br>
<h6>this is a level 6 heading</h6>
</body>
```

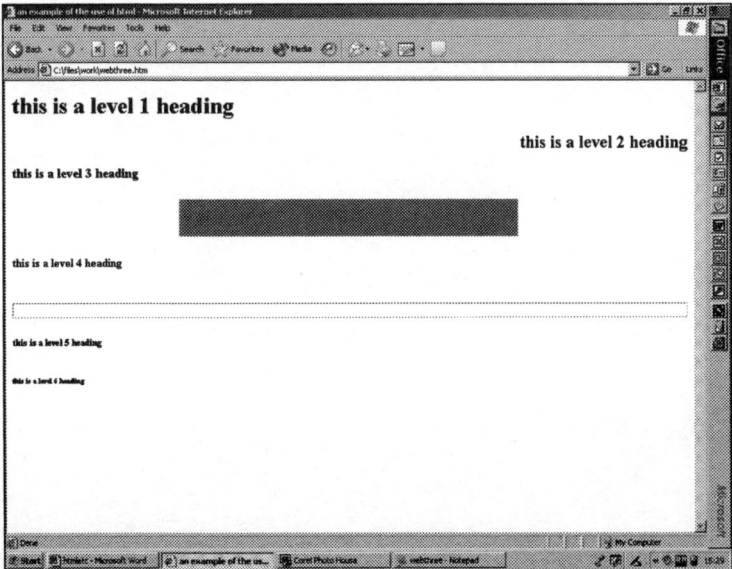

Exercise four

This exercise explores the code you have learnt so far and begins to build up your own home page.

☐   Create a new file, called **mypage.htm** and enter the example (on the next page). Enter paragraph or break tags as necessary.

title

my first home page

body

Change the font, the colour (e2380 is the hex code for red), centre this heading and make it heading level 2

Your name's home page

Heading level 4, in red and centred

created on date

revert to normal (default) text font and colour

Put in a solid horizontal line, size 10 pixels and 30% width of the page

heading level 4, colour red

address

revert to normal (default) text font and colour

type in your address using <br> to put each part of the address on a new line

there should be a new line for each part of the address

heading level 4, colour red

occupation

revert to normal (default) text and colour

type in your job title

Your page may look similar to this, although please experiment.

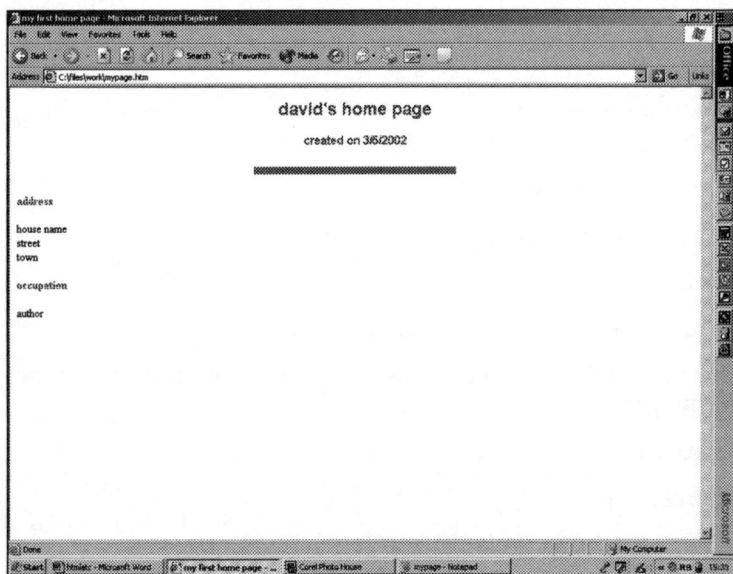

Note that the title does not appear in the page but is displayed in the title bar of the browser.

The coding for my page is as follows

```
<html><head><title>my first home page</title></head>
<body>
<font face=arial color=e2380>
<h2 align=center>
david's home page</h2>
<h4 align=center>
created on 26/11/99</h4>
</font></font>
<hr size=10 noshade width=30%>
<h4><font color=e2380>
address
</h4></font>
house name<br>
street<br>
town<br>
<postcode>
<p>
<h4><font color=e2380>
occupation
</h4></font>
author
</body></html>
```

Background colours

You have already looked at the coding for text colours, it is just as easy to alter the background.

<body background="file">

This uses a picture as the background. The file should be in a GIF format and stored in the same directory as the page.

<body bgcolor="nnnnnn">

The hex value to alter the background colour from white.

<body text="nnnnnn">

Again this is a hex code and alters the body text colour.

You use this for the majority of the text and then **<font color=>** to alter the colour of text within the page, when you close the **</font>**, the colour of the text will revert back to the **<body text>** setting.

Exercise five

☐　　Open the file **mypage.htm** and alter the body text colour to a kind of green (*hex: 21ca2*) and the background to light yellow (*hex: f2f4c6*).

Note how the headings remain in red as you used the **font color** tag to set them, which overwrites **<body text>**.

Adding graphics to your pages

You can include any graphic you wish, a company logo or a scanned picture of you and your family or employees.

The code for adding a graphic is:

<img src="image.gif">

An important aspect of graphics is that they have to be in certain file formats, i.e. .GIF or .JPG. You will have to convert your file to one of these formats using a program such as **Paint Shop Pro**.

You have some control over the position of the graphics on your pages. The following tags **align the text to the image** (not to the page as in <p align=center>).

align=top (or bottom or middle)

This code is included within the IMG tag, e.g.

<img src="image.gif" align=middle>

The effect of the tag will depend upon whether the text is before or after the image in your coding.

There are many sites on the Internet offering images (including animated gifs), mostly free.

Using the Alt tag

For text only browsers, you should include the <**alt**> tag to display text instead of a picture for those using out of date browsers.

<**img src="image.gif" alt="the picture shows an image of a cat"**>

Image dimensions, space and borders

The following tags define (in pixels) the size of the image on your page, the white space around the image and put a border (size in pixels) around the image.

White space means space between the graphic and the text or margin, it is not necessarily white.

The number of pixels on the screen is determined by the resolution of your screen, thus if you are using 800*600 resolution, this is the number of pixels on the screen.

width=nn height=nn (can also be a % of screen)

hspace=nn vspace=nn

An example:

<**img src="image.gif" width=200 height=300**>

Exercise six

Find an image you like and convert it into **gif** format, saving it into the same folder as your web pages.

☐ Add this to your own home page **mypage.htm,** adding the code to the line beneath the first heading on your page (Your name home page) and format it as follows:

☐ Size the image width and height 80 pixels.

☐ Put 20 pixels of white space above and below the image.

☐ Now align the image to the centre (you will need to use the **<p align=center>** to achieve this.

Here is an example of the additional coding:

```
<h2 align=center>
david's home page</h2>
<p align=center>
<img src=weale.gif width=80 height=80 vspace=20 >
```

At this point, your page should resemble that shown below.

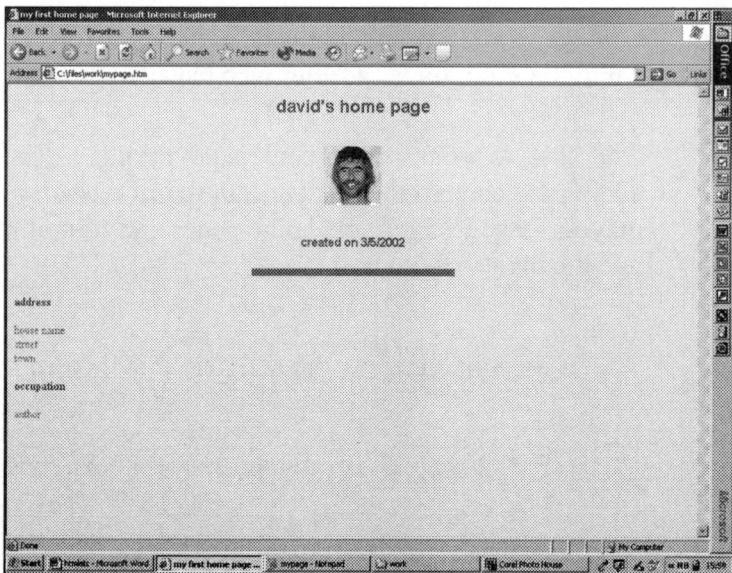

Once you have the general idea, it is time to experiment, save each of these changes and view them in the browser before proceeding to the next.

☐   Now alter the white space to 40 pixels and again the effect changes.

☐   Alter the vertical white space measurement to zero and yet again look at the changes.

☐   Alter the horizontal rule size to 3.

Exercise seven

☐ Using the same file, move the line of code (for the image) above the first heading and align the image to the right.

☐ Remove the centring for the headings and align the horizontal line to the left.

Your page should now look like this.

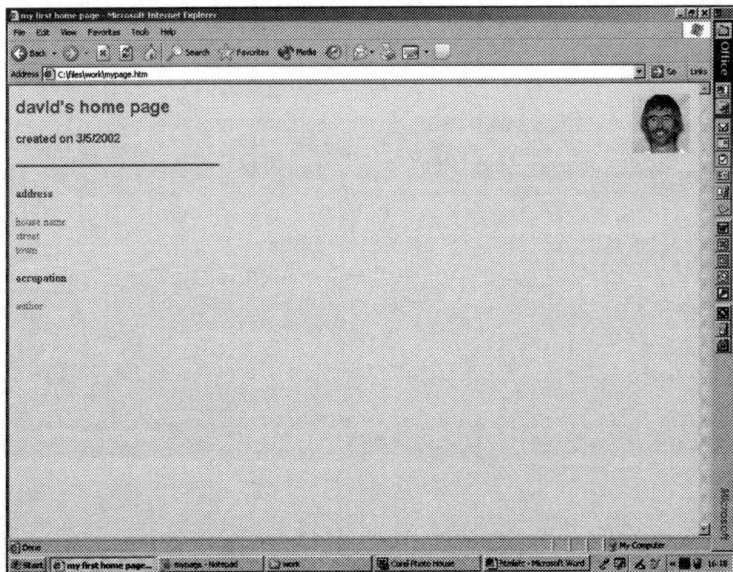

Exercise eight

☐ The next step is to produce another page, which you can call **pagetwo.htm**.

☐ This should contain details of the business address, telephone, a synopsis of its business activities and a contact name.

☐ Lay this out as you wish using the tags that have been covered so far (you do **not** need to use all of them).

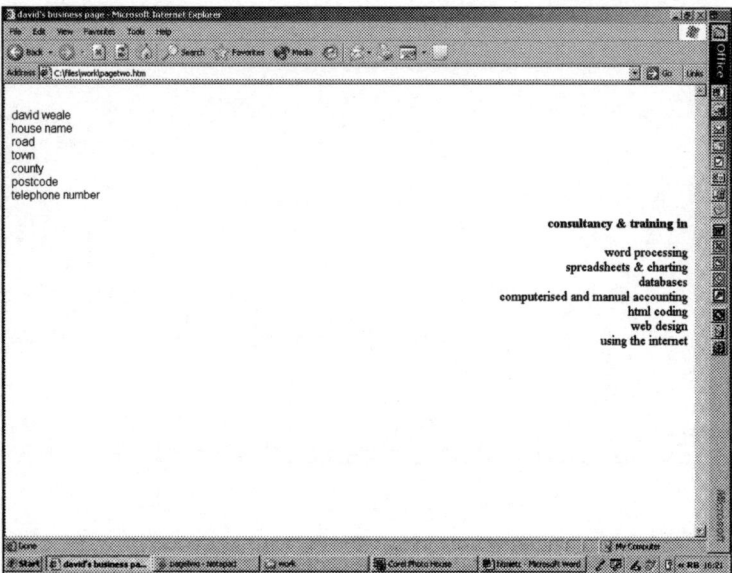

```
<html>
<head> <title>david's business page </title> </head>
<body>
<basefont size=4>
<pre><font face=arial>
david weale
house name
road
town
county
postcode
telephone number
</pre></font>
<font face=times new roman>
<h3 align=right>consultancy & training in</h3>
<p align=right>
word processing<br>
spreadsheets & charting<br>
databases<br>
computerised and manual accounting<br>
html coding<br>
web design<br>
using the internet<br>
</font>
</body>
</html>
```

Linking pages

You can create text links and/or graphics links to other pages (these links can be to another of your pages or to pages on another site).

Text links

The coding for these is:

\<a href="url">text explaining the link\</a>

The **a** stands for an anchor and is an integral part of the syntax. The URL is the address of the file you are linking to (whether on your hard disc or on the Internet).

Please remember to include some text, otherwise you will have a link but nothing will appear on the page.

E-mail links

If you want the reader to email you, you have to use a special hypertext link:

\<a href=mailto:your_email_address>anytext\</a>

Exercise nine

☐   Now to link the two pages together, start with **mypage.htm** and place the text link at the bottom of the page.

☐   The URL will be the address of your second file **pagetwo.htm**.

An example of the code is shown below (I have added the break tags to create space before the link).

```
<br><br>
<a href=pagetwo.htm>goto the second page</a>
```

Then open **pagetwo.htm** and insert a text link at the bottom of that page back to the first file.

When you browse either of these files, you should be able to click on the link and go directly to the other page. If this happens you have been successful.

Adding email links

Add an email link to **pagetwo.htm** (make up an email address if necessary e.g. davew@someisp.co.uk.

An example of the code:

```
<a href=mailto:davew@someisp.co.uk>email me</a>
```

Graphics links

To use graphics as a link simply include a reference to the graphic within the hypertext code, i.e.

<a href="mypage.htm"> <img src="arrow.gif"> click here or on the arrow to move to the previous page **</a>**

Exercise ten

☐   Add a graphic link to your file **pagetwo.htm** (at the bottom) replacing the original text link.

An example of the coding is shown below:

```
<a href=mypage.htm><img src=arrow.gif height=30 width=100
align=left></a>
```

You will need a graphic called **arrow.gif**. You can draw one in Microsoft Paint or any graphics program if you do not have a ready-made one.

Below is an example of how the second page could look.

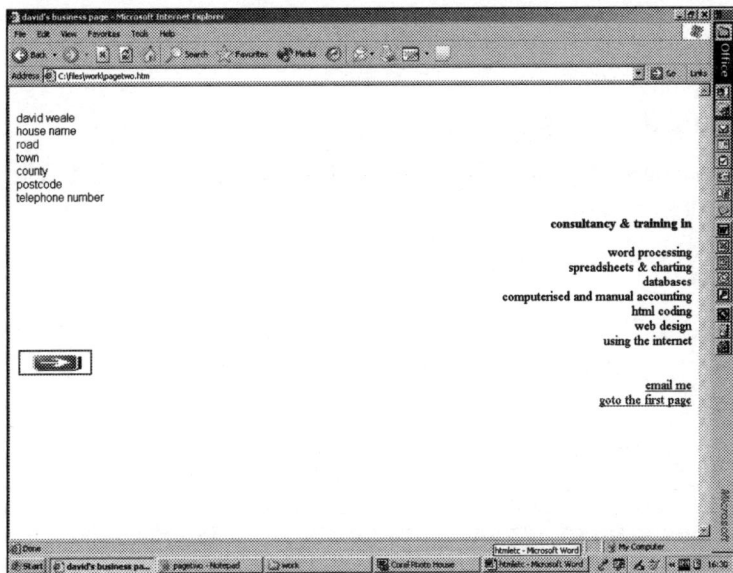

Lists

You may want to create lists of items.

Unordered lists

Unordered lists display bullets on each line of the list. The code for these is:

\<ul\>

\<li\>

\</ul\>

the **\<li\>** tag must appear before every item in the list.

If you want to introduce different style of bullets then

\<ul type="square" or "disc" or "circle"\>

will produce square or disc bullets instead of round ones (though not necessarily in all browsers).

Ordered lists

Ordered lists are numbered lists:

\<ol\>

\<li\>

\</ol\>

Nested lists

You can have lists within lists if you so wish (both numbered and bulleted lists).

```
<ul type="circle">
<li>this is a list of music I like
<li>billie holiday
<li>t-bone walker
<li>big joe turner
<li>jimmy rushing
<ul>
<li>a nested list begins here of other musicians
<li>louis jordan
<li>etta james
<li>ray charles
</ul>
</ul>
```

To begin a nested list simply start with another <ul> or <ol> **without** closing the original list.

Be careful to close the list with the closing tag </ul> or </ol> and enter this tag as many times as there are nests.

There are various changes you can make to numbered (ordered) lists.

Changing the numbering of ordered lists

<ol start=n>

Changes the start number for the list.

<li value=n>

Alters the number from that line.

<ol type=i>

Produces roman numeral type numbers. Also I, a, A can be used.

Using lists for links

You can create a list for your links if you want.

<ol>

<li><a href="http://www.yeovil-college.ac.uk>visit the Yeovil college site**</a>**

</ol>

Exercise eleven

☐ Create a file containing **both** an unordered (bulleted) list and an ordered (numbered) list. Ensure that you have included nested lists for both.

☐ The content of the lists can be anything you wish (if you have no ideas, perhaps you could produce a list similar to mine). Call the file **lists.htm**.

Below is an example of lists.

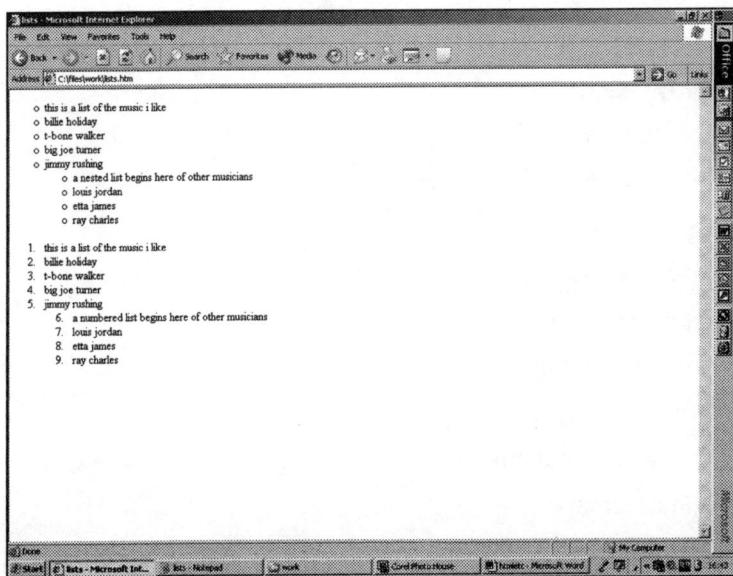

```
<html> <head> <title>lists</title></head>
<body>
<ul type="circle">
<li>this is a list of the music i like
<li>billie holiday
<li>t-bone walker
<li>big joe turner
<li>jimmy rushing
<ul>
<li>a nested list begins here of other musicians
<li>louis jordan
<li>etta james
<li>ray charles
</ul> </ul> <ol>
<li>this is a list of the music i like
<li>billie holiday
<li>t-bone walker
<li>big joe turner
<li>jimmy rushing
<ol>
<li value=6>a numbered list begins here of other musicians
<li>louis jordan
<li>etta james
<li>ray charles
</ol> </ol>
</body> </html>
```

Tables

Very useful and worth persevering with as they enable you to lay your pages out in an organised way. You can include text and/or graphics in the tables.

The tags

<table> </table>

The start and end of the table.

<td> </td>

Each item (i.e. a cell) is enclosed within these tags (each of these defines the column).

<tr> </tr>

Defines a row. You begin with a row, entering the columns and data for that row, then close that row and begin on the next row and so on.

Table borders

To make your table look impressive, you can add formatting. The codes are included within the <table> tag.

border=n (pixels)

cellspacing=n

cellpadding=n

An example of the coding and the subsequent table are shown below.

```
<body>
<h4>this is a table !</h4>
<table border=15 cellspacing=15 cellpadding=5>
<tr>
<td>row one, column one of the table</td>
<td>column two</td>
<td>column three</td>
</tr>
<tr>
<td>row two, column one of the table</td>
<td>column two</td>
<td>column three</td>
</tr>
</table>
</body>
```

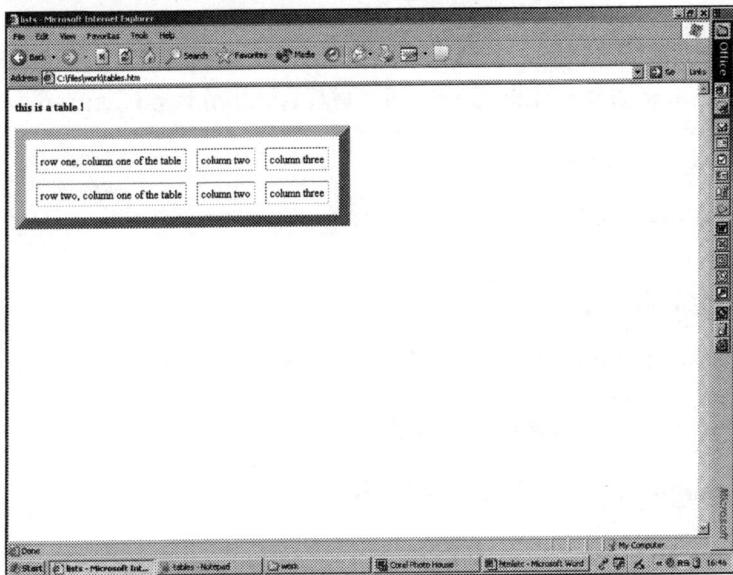

Additional table tags

Table captions

If you want to include a caption explaining the table, use the following tags.

\<caption\> text \</caption\>

You can alter the font and so on by adding the necessary code, e.g.

\<caption font size=5\>

Table headings

Similar to the <td> tag but the text is in bold and centred.

The tags are:

<th> </th>

Aligning text in tables

You can align text using the following additional code.

align=left or center or right

valign=top or middle or bottom

(align aligns text horizontally, valign aligns vertically within the cells).

colspan=2

This merges two rows into one.

width=n

This defines the width of the column or table (in pixels or %).

Instead of text, you can include a link or a graphic.

Exercise twelve

Create a file containing a table of five rows and two columns with a caption, call the file **net.htm**.

The contents of the table should be as follows:

Using the NET

Information Providers	Fixed Charge per month
Demon	Yes
Virgin Net	Yes/Variable
AOL	Variable
CompuServe	Variable

Format the table in various ways until you are happy with the result.

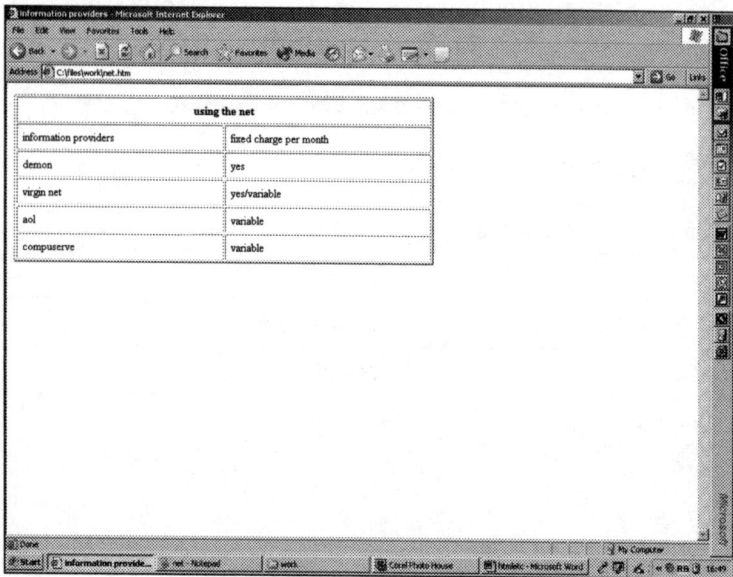

```
<html><head><title>information providers</title></head>
<body>
<table border=2 cellspacing=2 cellpadding=7 width=590>
<tr><td valign="middle" colspan=2>
<b><p align="center">using the net</b></td></tr>
<tr><td width="50%" valign="top">
<p>information providers</td>
<td width="50%" valign="top">
<p>fixed charge per month</td></tr>
<tr><td width="50%" valign="top">
<p>demon</td>
<td width="50%" valign="top">
<p>yes</td></tr>
<tr><td width="50%" valign="top">
<p>virgin net</td>
<td width="50%" valign="top">
<p>yes/variable</td></tr>
<tr><td width="50%" valign="top">
<p>aol</td>
<td width="50%" valign="top">
<p>variable</td></tr>
<tr><td width="50%" valign="top">
<p>compuserve</td>
<td width="50%" valign="top">
<p>variable</td></tr>
</table></body></html>
```

Designing web sites

First thoughts

Decide upon what you are trying to achieve and whom you are targeting. What do you think people will want from your site?

Look at other sites, especially your competitors.

Always draw a diagram of how the site is to be structured before beginning any coding. You can always alter it later. Planning efficiently at this stage will save hours of work later.

Try to think yourself into the same mindset as potential viewers.

Copyright

Copyright applies to web pages as much as it does to printed material (as do the laws of defamation and so on).

General design tips

Write concisely, clearly, and **simply**.

Always test your pages exhaustively for sense, spelling, grammar, layout and links and then test them again!

Test them in both MS Explorer and Netscape, some designers create two sets of pages, each set optimised for one of the browsers.

If you leave the most important material to the end of the page there is a possibility that the reader will not get that far.

Try to avoid the need for the reader to scroll (better to start a new page using hypertext links from one to the other or use links within the page or frames).

Whether to use frames?

Think carefully before using frames; certainly avoid complex frame layouts as it can be difficult to navigate around sites containing too many frames.

On the other hand, frames are a useful way to let the user navigate around your site. Using them means that the viewer has fewer mouse clicks to arrive at any point and they can see the various choices all the time.

However recently they have fallen out of favour for the following reasons.

❑ They can confuse search engines.

❑ Only part of the screen is used for the actual content.

❑ Some (older) browsers find it difficult to print or save frame pages.

Backgrounds and fonts

Be very careful if you want to use textured or coloured backgrounds to your pages, they can make the text more difficult to read. Similarly avoid irritating sounds.

Keep the design simple and do not use more than two or three fonts or colours on any page.

Links

Links should contain a description explaining why the viewer may want to look at them.

Make it obvious what text and pictures are links so that the reader is clear where to click the mouse.

Always and **regularly** check the links you have created (both internal and external), nothing is more irritating than broken links.

Text

Black text on a white background is traditional (after all this is how books have been produced for centuries), if you feel this is too boring then try dark colours on a light background and so on.

If you reverse the colours (e.g. white text on a black background) then it may be difficult to read and to print on paper.

Blinking text (or pages) is bad news and scrolling text (marquees) and animations can become tiresome quickly and may not display properly in all browsers or screens.

Experiment, but always test new ideas with a sample of your intended audience.

Minimising file size and increasing speed

You need to experiment to get the best balance between image file size (and consequent download time) and quality of image.

You can alter the resolution, number of colours or file type to get the best compromise from the file format you are using.

Never assume that your readers are using a visual browser (even if they have a state of the art browser they may have turned off the images for speed), always use an <**img alt**="text"> so that the reader knows what they are missing.

Remember that large files take time to download and the viewer can get irritated quickly (especially if they are paying the telephone bills). Try to avoid long download times as the viewer may click the **STOP** button. Large graphics can slow the download times.

It is recommended that the initial page should download quickly (less than 10-15 seconds at average download speeds).

Site Structure

Divide your site into a series of pages, each with a link to the next and previous and organise them in a coherent and logical way.

Each page should be independent of the others (and contain links to your home page) since the user may have jumped to a page on your site that is not your home page.

There is a concept called the 3-click rule, this says that no page should be more than three mouse clicks away.

You should also try to avoid confusing the reader by giving them too many buttons to click on any one page (possibly six is a good maximum).

Reverse engineering

Spend some time looking around the Net at the way in which pages and sites are constructed. You will learn much; some are good, some bad.

I suggest you look at the source code of the pages you find attractive. There is nothing wrong with adapting other people's ideas; this is very different from plagiarism.

Remember there are very few geniuses; most of us make do with a little inspiration and a lot of hard work.

Getting readers for your site

Include your URL in all company literature (letters, invoices, advertising, etc.).

Maintain the site by checking the contents regularly and update the information **and links** (out of date information is a quick way to kill interest in a site), to make your site interesting, add new material regularly.

Use forms and/or counters to analyse the response to the site.

Include your E-mail address and if you are expecting a response from abroad remember to include your international dialling code for telephone or fax replies.

Will your pages be found?

Get your site included in as many search engines as possible as long as they are relevant to your site and are likely to be used by your potential viewers.

In practice this means the major engines plus any minor engines that deal with your type of subject matter and/or geographic region.

It is preferable to submit your site yourself to the major engines rather than rely on the automated submission services.

It is worthwhile submitting not just your index page but also the two or three pages that best epitomise what your site is about in case the search engines have problems reading the index page.

Normally the search engines will follow the links to the remainder of your pages, indexing as they go.

There will be a time delay between submitting your URL and your pages being indexed, this can be several weeks so be patient.

It is worthwhile re-registering whenever you make major changes to your site, as it may be some time before the engines revisit your site.

Keywords

Search engines do not always index the same type of material, for example, some index the contents of **meta** tags and others do not.

Some engines list the page title in searches so it is important to have a title that is understandable and clearly explains the purpose of your page.

Search engines decide how high to rank your pages based upon the placement and frequency of keywords.

Including keywords in the following places can increase your ranking with some search engines.

❑ TITLE tag

❑ Keyword & Description Meta tags

❑ First 25 words of body text

❑ In <! Comments tags

❑ Inside <ALT> tags

❑ Inside NO FRAMES tags

You are more likely to get a high listing if your keywords are two (or more) words long. This is simply because single words are likely to occur in too many pages and your pages are therefore competing with too many other pages.

Where you position the keywords is of importance. It is vital that the **title** tag includes your primary keywords as most search engines use this.

Try to use keywords in headings and as high up the page as possible as search engines will give them more importance.

Look at the source code for highly ranked sites, seeing how they use keywords to obtain a high ranking.

While tables are a useful layout technique, they can make keywords included within them appear of less relevance (simply because of the way in which search engines read tables). Some search engines will not read image maps or links contained within frames.

Meta tags

The **description** Meta tag appears in the place of the summary the search engine would normally print in the search results.

The **keyword** meta tag should include any keywords you want the search engine to associate with your page.

The keyword meta tag provides keywords to match with the words the viewer types in when using the search engine.

When creating the keywords **meta tags**, think about the kind of keywords you would use if you were searching for information similar to that contained within your web page.

An example of how to use meta tags is shown below.

```
<html>
<head>
<meta name="description" content="computer training & problem solving">
<meta name="keywords" content="lecturer, writing web pages, computer advice">
<title>david weale's business page
</title>
</head>
<body>make sure you include keywords within the content of your page, although this is unlikely to be a problem
</body>
</html>
```

Search engines that make use of Meta tags will display the following descriptions, the first line from the title tag and the second from the description Meta tag.

```
david weale's business page
computer training & problem solving
```

Glossary

Archie	A program to find on-line material - an older form of retrieval, superseded by the WWW
Backbone	The infrastructure of the internet, data travels from one network to another via the backbone
Bandwidth	How much data can be sent along a connection
Baud rate	Measures the speed of data travelling along communication lines, measured in KBPS (kilobytes per second)
Browser	The program that enables you to view HTML documents (both on-line and off-line)
Dial-up	Connect to the Net
Domain	The address of the host computer
Download	Transfer data from a web site to your computer
E-mail	Electronic mail - you have an e-mail address in a similar way to your home address

FAQ	Frequently asked question, many sites have a list of FAQs so you can learn the basics about the site
Flame	An e-mail (not nice) sent to the originator of a message. It has been known for thousands of people to flame a particular site, jamming the server
FTP	File Transfer Protocol - a quick way of transferring files from one Net site to another
Gopher	Means 'Go For' - a method of finding the information you require using a menu system - the antecedent of the WWW
Home page	The first page for a site (normally Index.htm)
HTML	Hypertext mark-up language - the code in which web pages are written
HTTP	Hypertext transfer protocol (how HTML documents get transferred around the Net)
Hypertext link	A link from one web page to another, it can be text or a graphic

Intranet	An internal (company) internet using the same protocols, it makes accessing company-wide data easy and cheap compared with traditional methods (only one copy of documents exist and they are held centrally on the server)
JavaScript	A programming language for internet applications
Modem	Modulator/demodulator - hardware that translates digital data into analogue and back again (so the data can travel the telephone system)
Netiquette	Behave or you will be flamed
Newsgroup	A Usenet discussion group
On-line	Connected to the Net and using the telephone lines; off-line means using Net tools, e.g. browsers without being connected
POP	Point of presence
Plug-ins	Additional programs for web browsers
Server	The computer which hosts the web site

Snail mail	Traditional physical post systems
Spam	Sending a message to many Usenet newsgroups - normally a breach of Netiquette (you may get flamed as a result)
Telnet	Allows you to take control of a remote computer - obviously access is restricted to certain public sites
URL	Uniform Resource Locator - the address
Winsock	A Windows file that enables Windows to communicate with the Net servers
WWW	World Wide Web

Index

Z

Notes